WHAT THE CHURCH TEACHES ABOUT

Sex

WHAT THE CHURCH TEACHES ABOUT

Sex

GOD'S PLAN FOR HUMAN HAPPINESS

ROBERT L. FASTIGGI, PH.D.

Our Sunday Visitor Publishing Division
Our Sunday Visitor, Inc.
Huntington, Indiana 46750

Nihil Obstat
Rev. Msgr. John P. Zenz, S.T.D.
Censor Deputatus

Imprimatur
His Eminence, Adam Cardinal Maida
Archbishop of Detroit
April 29, 2008

The *Nihil Obstsat* and *Imprimatur* are declarations that a work is free from doctrinal or moral error. It is not implied that those who have granted the *Nihil Obstat* and *Imprimatur* agree with the contents, opinions, or statements expressed.

Unless otherwise noted, Scripture citations contained in this work are taken from the *Catholic Edition of the Revised Standard Version of the Bible* (RSV), copyright © 1965 and 1966 by the Division of Christian Education of the National Council of the Churches of Christ in the United States of America. Used by permission. All rights reserved.

Excerpts from the *Catechism of the Catholic Church, Second Edition*, for use in the United States of America, copyright © 1994 and 1997, United States Catholic Conference — Libreria Editrice Vaticana. Used by permission. All rights reserved.

Every reasonable effort has been made to determine copyright holders of excerpted materials and to secure permissions as needed. If any copyrighted materials have been inadvertently used in this work without proper credit being given in one form or another, please notify Our Sunday Visitor in writing so that future printings of this work may be corrected accordingly.

Our Sunday Visitor Publishing Division
Our Sunday Visitor, Inc.
200 Noll Plaza
Huntington, IN 46750

ISBN 978-1-59276-212-5 (Inventory No. T263)
LCCN: 2008925253

Cover design by Lindsey Luken
Interior design by Sherri L. Hoffman
Cover photo by Shutterstock

PRINTED IN THE UNITED STATES OF AMERICA

*To my wife, Kathy,
and our three children:
Mary, Anthony, and Clare.*

CONTENTS

Among the students and faculty at Sacred Heart Major Seminary, Prof. Robert Fastiggi is known as a man with a sincere and deep love for the Church and her wisdom. For Fastiggi, the best reason to perform an action is because the Church approves the action, and the best reason to reject an evil action is because the Church teaches that it is evil. Fastiggi profoundly believes that Christ is with his Church and that the Church is guided by the Holy Spirit. Fastiggi also, of course, understands that natural law is a source of wisdom in respect to action. In this book, he explains the natural law justifications for the Church's moral teaching and also draws upon the deliverances of modern science that support those teachings. Nonetheless, one senses that his interest in natural law and science is motivated a great deal by the fact that the Church honors natural law and science; for Fastiggi, it is the Church that should be the foremost guide for all our pursuits. Not because he has loyalty to an institution as some people have loyalty to their college or their sports team, but because he knows that the Church and Christ are one and that in following the Church he is more truly following Christ.

Among his colleagues and students, Fastiggi is also known as the "source guy," the one to go to if one wants to know what the Church has taught on this or that issue. In this book, in keeping with his devotion to the Church, Fastiggi turns to Church documents to explain sexual morality — both those of the distant past and also very contemporary ones. Many Catholics do not understand that Christ promised us that in his absence he would continue to guide the Church through the power of the Holy Spirit; when the Church teaches, we are hearing the voice of Christ himself. Disobedience to the Church and rejection of Church teaching amounts to a rejection of Christ himself. Those unaccustomed to consulting magisterial documents will likely be surprised at the wisdom that these documents contain — and will likely be much more inclined in the future to enjoy turning to magisterial documents, such as the *Catechism* and encyclicals, for wisdom and inspiration as well as guidance.

The reader will also be able to watch a theologian at work, as Fastiggi occasionally explores and resolves debates such as the teaching that procreation is the primary end of marriage. The reader will be guided through intricate deliberations by theologians and evolving and carefully nuanced statements by the magisterium. Some readers will find following this discussion somewhat like reading a mystery novel. Others may not find such debates of tremendous interest; they likely will find their questions answered more directly in the chapters dealing with specific moral acts.

Fastiggi uses the interesting and captivating technique of beginning chapters with a recounting of some conversation he had that reveals some fundamental misunderstanding of Church teaching. With his characteristic charity, patience, and thoroughness, he reveals the likely reasons for the misunderstanding and then turns to authoritative statements of the Church to explain what the Church really teaches. In the chapters on specific moral issues, such as pornography and masturbation, he not only draws upon the wisdom of magisterial teaching, he also refers to the supporting studies from modern psychological and sociological science. The reader will find an abundance of useful sources to supplement the text. Fastiggi offers sound practical advice for those suffering from temptation to and practice of various sexual sins.

Indeed, Fastiggi begins his work with a recounting of St. Augustine's struggle with sexual sin. Augustine's was not a momentary adolescent succumbing to sexual sin, but a prolonged and repeated violation of morality. His resistance to following Church teaching was fierce, but finally, as his intellectual understanding of the Church and morality advanced and as he became more open to the power of grace, he was able to radically change his thinking about sexuality and his sexual behavior, and he eventually attained sainthood.

Given the fact that most Catholics now have sex before marriage and engage in many other sexual sins such as the use of pornography and contraception, Fastiggi is wise to begin with this story of a reformed sinner who became one of the greatest saints of the Church. Fastiggi's repeated message that repentance and conversion and a changed lifestyle are possible is very reassuring. Sadly, one of the reasons that so many Catholics fall into such serious sexual sin is that they do not know the teaching of the Church on sexual matters. They do not respect the Church as a teacher, and they do not know the reasons why the Church teaches what it teaches. Augustine's moral conversion began with an intellectual conversion — a conversion of understanding what the truth is and the importance of living by it. That understanding led him to ask for the grace to live by the truth. Readers of this book may well find themselves undergoing a similar conversion process — to the truth itself, to the necessity of asking for grace, and to the joy of being a member of the Catholic Church.

Dr. Janet E. Smith

THE GOOD NEWS ABOUT SEX: GOD WISHES HAPPINESS FOR HIS CHILDREN

Back in the early 1970s, I was a student at Dartmouth College in New Hampshire. I remember taking a literature class in which we were assigned to read *A Portrait of the Artist as a Young Man*, by James Joyce. The class was team-taught, and one professor commented on Joyce's struggle between his instinctual sense of the goodness of sex and the very negative view of sexuality taught by his Catholic religion.

I understood how Joyce's novel could lead to the impression conveyed, but I was, nonetheless, disturbed. I decided to visit the professor during his office hour. I politely told him that I was Catholic and that I found his generality about sex and Catholicism unfair. The professor, who was a gracious man, smiled and said, "But how could anyone not acknowledge Catholicism's negative view of sex?" I calmly replied, "But if that is so, why does the Catholic Church look upon marriage as a sacrament?" The professor was a bit stunned by my comment. It took him a while to reply, and when he did, he said, "I see your point, and I'll give it some consideration, but I was thinking about the Catholic Church's negative view of sex *outside* of marriage."

This conversation sticks in my mind after more than thirty years because the professor was a victim of a sad but common misconception. Many people think the Catholic Church is "against sex" because she opposes sex outside of marriage. This, though, is very superficial reasoning. The reservation of sexual intimacy to the marriage covenant is actually due to a deep reverence for the sanctity and goodness of human sexuality and its natural connection to the procreation and education of children.

Unfortunately, the true beauty and dignity of sexual intimacy has become debased in contemporary culture. It is interesting that the vulgar four-letter word associated with the sexual act is often used to express anger. In fact, I once heard a man, upset over a near traffic accident, use variations of this word as a verb, an adjective, and a noun in a single sentence! But if sexual intimacy is truly beautiful and good, why do so many people use a vulgar word for it to express anger?

The vulgar and crude way many people speak of sex is, I believe, a reflection of an inward sense of impurity. Deep down, they know they have taken sex out of its sacral context, so they need to debase it in their speech. How different is the language of the Catholic Church, which looks upon sexual union in marriage as something "noble and honorable" which fosters self-giving and "enriches the spouses in joy and gratitude."[1] Indeed, the Church describes marital love as one that brings together "the human and the divine" and "leads the partners to a free and mutual giving of self, experienced in tenderness and action," which "permeates their whole lives."[2] Moreover, the sexual act is linked by nature to human procreation wherein the spouses cooperate with God in bringing forth new human life.

The Catholic understanding of sex is "glad tidings" or "good news" for our times. In many respects, our contemporary culture has distorted the true meaning of sex. The "sexual revolution" begun in the 1960s and 1970s has injured many people and con-

---

[1] Cf. Vatican II, *Gaudium et Spes*, 49; translation taken from Austin Flannery, O.P., *Vatican II: The Conciliar and Post Conciliar Documents*, New Revised Edition (Boston, MA: St. Paul Books & Media, 1992), 952; all subsequent citations will be taken from this volume.

[2] Ibid.

tinues to do so. Some of the harms can be quantified in terms of escalating rates of divorce, venereal disease, abortion, and illegitimacy.[3] These realities are linked to other social wounds — children injured by marital breakups, boys and girls deprived of fatherly or motherly care, domestic violence, the psychological and physical scars of abortion, people abused as objects of sexual gratification, and the heartaches of broken relationships.

What has led to this state of affairs? To some extent, it is a return to godlessness and paganism, for in the ancient Greco-Roman culture, prostitution and sexual promiscuity were widespread.[4] It might also be linked to the growth of secularism, a movement away from traditional religious norms that began in the Enlightenment of the eighteenth century. Others see the sexual revolution as a logical outgrowth of the birth control pill and other forms of contraception. Once the connection between sex and procreation is severed, the conjugal act need not take place within marriage, since sexual pleasure can be pursued apart from the context of committed love and babies. And if sexual intercourse can be enjoyed outside of marriage, the way is open to other forms of genital indulgence: mutual masturbation, oral sex, and anal sex — whether heterosexual or homosexual.

The sexual revolution is viewed as a departure from God's plan for human happiness and flourishing — not only by Catholics, but by many other Christians, as well as numerous Jews, Muslims, and adherents of diverse faiths. If we believe in God, we trust that God has a purpose in mind for His creation. The Bible tells us that

---

[3] According to the National Center for Health Statistics of the U.S. Department of Health and Human Services, 10.7 percent of U.S. children were born to unmarried mothers in 1970; by 2002, this figure had gone up to 34% for all races and 68.2% for blacks; cf. *The World Almanac and Book of Facts* (New York: World Almanac Books, 2006), 181. The negative social effects of cohabitation, divorce, and unmarried childbearing are also documented in W. Bradford Wilcox, *Why Marriage Matters: Twenty-Six Conclusions from the Social Sciences*, 2nd Edition (New York: Institute for American Values, 2005).

[4] Cf. Rev. Ronald Lawler, O.F.M. Cap., Joseph Boyle, Jr., and William E. May, *Catholic Sexual Ethics: A Summary, Explanation & Defense*, Second Edition (Huntington, IN, 1998), 47; Sexual license among the ancient Romans is also witnessed to by St. Paul in Rom 1:24–27.

after the six days of creation, "And God saw everything that he had made, and behold, it was very good" (Gen 1:31). In Gen 1:26–27, we read that God created man in His image and after His likeness; He created human beings male and female, and then He blessed them, saying: "Be fruitful and multiply and fill the earth and subdue it" (Gen 1:28).

There is much revealed to us in these few verses. It is God's will for human beings to be male and female and to procreate. Moreover, these activities are "very good" and even "godlike" because human beings are created in the image and likeness of God. In the second chapter of Genesis, we read how God realized that "it is not good that the man should be alone" (Gen 2:18). None of the other animals proves to be a "suitable partner" for the man, so God casts a deep sleep on the man, and He forms the woman, the suitable partner, out of his side. The woman is "bone of his bones and flesh of his flesh" (cf. Gen 2:23). She and the man are made for each other — to "become one flesh" (Gen 2:24) as husband and wife.

Scripture reveals the fundamental design and purpose of human sexuality in its opening chapters. Man and woman are created in God's image and likeness to "be fruitful and multiply" and to unite as one flesh in marriage. These two purposes constitute the procreative and the unitive ends of marriage, and they reveal God's design for the sexual act. According to Pope Paul VI, there is "an unbreakable connection between the unitive meaning and the procreative meaning"[5] of the conjugal act. Moreover, this "connection was established by God, and Man is not permitted to break it through his own volition."[6]

This essential connection between sexual union and the capacity to bring forth new life is perfectly reasonable. God knows that children develop best when they have a loving father and mother who are united in the stable bond of matrimony. The Catholic un-

---

[5] Paul VI, Encyclical Letter, *Humanae Vitae*, 12; translation taken from Janet E. Smith, *Humanae Vitae: A Generation Later* (Washington, D.C.: Catholic University of America Press, 1991), 281.

[6] Ibid.

derstanding of human sexuality, therefore, is in accord with both divine revelation and natural reason. The removal of sexual intimacy from the stability of committed married love has dire social consequences. Bernard Nathanson, M.D., the one-time abortionist turned pro-life leader, puts the matter well:

> Pregnancy and childbirth are cohesive in their effect on the family, while sex apart from the family and childbearing is never socially cohesive; on the contrary, it is a chaotic force.[7]

Is sex outside of marriage a chaotic force? There is much evidence to suggest that it is. Those who look upon sex as simply pleasure or recreation are ignoring reality. When a child is conceived from an act of pleasure or exploitation, he or she is not willed as a good but is looked upon as an unfortunate consequence. All the condoms, diaphragms, and birth control pills available in modern culture have not eliminated the reality of unwanted pregnancies. As a result, unborn children are killed through abortion or brought into the world deprived of the stability of married parents.[8]

The denial of the natural connection between sexual union and procreation is also the result of a distorted understanding of the human body and human relations. As Pope John Paul II writes:

> Within this same cultural climate, the body is no longer perceived as a properly personal reality, a sign and place of relations with others, with God and the world. It is reduced to pure materiality: it is simply a complex of organs, functions and energies to be used according to the sole criteria of pleasure and efficiency. Consequently, sexuality too is depersonalized and exploited: from being the sign, place and language of love, that is, of the gift of self and acceptance of another in all the other's richness as a person, it increasingly becomes the occasion and the instrument for self-assertion and the selfish satisfaction of

---

[7] Bernard Nathanson, M.D., with Richard Ostling, *Aborting America* (Garden City, NY: Doubleday & Company, 1979), 257.

[8] See footnote 3.

personal desires and instincts. Thus the original import of human sexuality is distorted and falsified, and the two meanings, unitive and procreative, inherent in the very nature of the conjugal act are artificially separated: in this way the marriage union is betrayed and its fruitfulness is subjected to the caprice of the couple. Procreation then becomes the "enemy" to be avoided in sexual activity.[9]

Because sexual activity is frequently removed from its natural connection to marriage and procreation, it takes on a chaotic and tragic character. Instead of being an expression of authentic, self-giving love, sex becomes an expression of passionate desire or what the Greeks called *eros*. Pope Benedict XVI, in his encyclical, *Deus Caritas Est*, notes that:

> The Greeks — not unlike other cultures — considered *eros* principally as a kind of intoxication, the overpowering of reason by a "divine madness," which tears man away from his finite existence and enables him, in the very process of being overwhelmed by divine power, to experience supreme happiness.... In the religions, this attitude found expression in the fertility cults, part of which was the "sacred" prostitution which flourished in many temples. *Eros* was thus celebrated as divine power, as fellowship with the Divine.[10]

Pope Benedict notes that the Old Testament "firmly opposed this form of religion ... but it in no way rejected *eros* as such; rather it declared war on a warped and destructive form of it, because this counterfeit divinization of *eros* actually strips it of its dignity and dehumanizes it."[11] Indeed, to achieve "divine madness" by the sexual exploitation of women is hardly noble.

---

[9] John Paul II, Encyclical Letter, *Evangelium Vitae* [1995], 23: http://www.vatican.va_holy_father/john_paul_ii/encyclicals/hf_jp-ii_enc_25031995_evangelium.

[10] Benedict XVI, Encyclical Letter, *Deus Caritas Est* [Dec. 25, 2005], 4; published as a special supplement by *Inside the Vatican* magazine. When subsequent documents of the Magisterium are cited, the translations are from the Vatican Web site unless otherwise indicated.

[11] Ibid.

The dynamic power of *eros* — which moves human beings out of themselves in search of union — needs to be healed and purified. Because of original sin, human beings have a tendency to take something good, such as human sexuality, and abuse and disfigure it. Pope Benedict notes that Christianity "is often criticized as having been opposed to the body; and it is quite true that tendencies of this sort have existed."[12] But the contemporary, secular view often reduces *eros* to "pure sex ... a commodity, a mere 'thing' to be bought and sold."[13] As the Holy Father observes:

> Here we are actually dealing with a debasement of the human body: no longer is it integrated into our overall existential freedom; no longer is it a vital expression of our whole being, but it is more or less relegated to the purely biological sphere. The apparent exaltation of the body can quickly turn into a hatred of bodiliness. Christian faith, on the other hand, has always considered man a unity in duality, a reality in which spirit and matter compenetrate, and in which each is brought to a new nobility. True, *eros* tends to rise "in ecstasy" toward the Divine, to lead us beyond ourselves; yet for this very reason it calls for a path of ascent, renunciation, purification, and healing.[14]

The purpose of this book is to seek a purification of attitudes about sex by a presentation of the authentic Catholic understanding of this precious gift and its proper use. By examining the various aspects and questions related to human sexuality, I hope to show that the Catholic view of sex is in accord with reason, human nature, and the will of God (and all three of these should work together).

Underlying this hope is the concern for human happiness. Having been born in 1953, I fall into the "baby boom" generation of the post-World War II United States. In my young adult years, the "sexual revolution" was in full swing, and I observed its deleterious effects on our culture. Sadly, even the Catholic Church

---

[12] *Deus Caritas Est*, 5.
[13] Ibid.
[14] Ibid.

was not immune from this loosening of sexual morality. During the 1960s and 1970s, many Catholic priests and teachers began to take an indulgent attitude — first toward contraception in marriage — and then toward masturbation, premarital sex, homosexual actions, divorce, remarriage, and ultimately abortion.[15]

When there is a departure from the order of God's creation, human happiness is frustrated and suffering follows. Along these lines, I believe that many people, especially women, have been deeply injured by the sexual revolution (and the harm continues in many circles!). After women, I believe children have suffered the most from irresponsible sexual behavior, especially children who have grown up deprived of fatherly guidance and example. While the secular culture that surrounds us continues to promote a distorted understanding of sex, the Catholic Church, in her official teachings, has been remarkably consistent: sexual union — because of its intrinsic connection to procreation and the intimate love between a man and a woman — can take place morally only within sacred matrimony. From this fundamental moral principle, many other matters surrounding human sexuality become clear. This book, in its own modest way, will seek to explore these issues.

---

[15] While I hesitate to tell personal stories, I can report that, in 1976, while a graduate student of theology at Fordham University, a Catholic priest and professor of moral theology counseled me to become sexually active after I told him I was not. I have since learned that during this same period certain seminaries in the U.S.A. were requiring priest aspirants to watch graphic films depicting various homosexual and heterosexual acts. Others who lived through this period can, I'm sure, multiply stories such as these. We can only hope that the priests responsible for such erroneous judgments have since learned the errors of their ways and repented. Evidence of the decline of Catholic sexual morality during this period can be found in *Human Sexuality: New Directions in American Catholic Thought* (New York: Paulist Press, 1977) edited by Anthony Kosnik et al., which was commissioned by the Catholic Theological Society of America. Both the U.S. Bishops' Committee on Doctrine and the Congregation for the Doctrine of the Faith criticized this book.; cf. Austin Flannery, Austin, O.P. ed. *Vatican II: More Post Conciliar Documents* (Collegeville, MN: The Liturgical Press, 1982), 505–509.

CHAPTER ONE

THE STRUGGLE FOR CHASTITY:
THE CASE OF ST. AUGUSTINE

When I was a graduate student in theology at Fordham University in the late 1970s, I sat in on a class taught by the Franciscan priest, Fr. Benedict J. Groeschel. With his characteristic sense of humor, Father Benedict told the students that the Bronx[1] was the ideal place to study theology because there was so much empirical evidence for the existence of original sin.

Yet one need not live in the Bronx to see the effects of original sin. The *Catechism of the Catholic Church* defines original sin as "the deprivation of original holiness and justice."[2] This deprivation of the original holiness and justice (which included sanctifying grace) is what theologians call the "formal" aspect of original sin. After the fall, the human nature transmitted by our original parents was one "deprived of original holiness and justice."[3] Thus, original sin is a sin "only in an analogical sense: it is a sin 'contracted' and not 'committed' — a state and not an act."[4]

This formal aspect of original sin is erased by baptism from which we receive the life of grace merited for us by Christ's death and Resurrection. This is why the Council of Trent describes

---

[1] The Bronx is the part of New York City where the main campus of Fordham University is located.

[2] *Catechism of the Catholic Church*, Second Edition (Libreria Editrice Vaticana, 1997) [henceforth, CCC], no. 405.

[3] CCC 404.

[4] Ibid.

baptism as "the instrumental cause" of justification.[5] The sanctifying grace we receive at baptism erases the inherited deprivation known as original sin, but it does not remove its "material effects" that persist in our human nature. These effects are called "material" because they differ from the "formal" aspect of original sin, which is the deprivation of sanctifying grace. The *Catechism* is very clear on this point:

> Baptism, by imparting the life of Christ's grace, erases original sin and turns a man back to God, but the consequences for nature, weakened and inclined to evil, persist in man and summon him to spiritual battle.[6]

What are the material effects of original sin on our human nature? The *Catechism* explains that our "human nature has not been totally corrupted: it is wounded in the natural powers proper to it; subject to ignorance, suffering, and the dominion of death; and inclined to sin — an inclination that is called "concupiscence.""[7]

The word "concupiscence" (*concupiscentia*) comes from the Latin verb *concupiscere*, which means "to desire, to long for, to covet."[8] Because of original sin, we tend to covet things in a disordered way. St. John warns us that "all that is in the world, the lust of the flesh and the lust of the eyes and the pride of life, is not of the Father but is of the world" (1 Jn 2:16). Thus, concupiscence encompasses sensual lust, greed, envy, and pride. It can be understood as "the movement of the sensitive appetite, contrary to the operation of human reason."[9] While concupiscence is not sin in itself, it is the fuel or tinder for sin.[10] The *Catechism* explains that:

---

[5] Denzinger, Heinrich, and Peter Hünermann, *Enchiridion symbolorum definitionum et declarationum de rebus fidei et morum*, 40th ed. (Freiburg: Herder, 2005) [henceforth, Denz.-H], no. 152; all translations from Denz.-H and other Latin texts are my own unless otherwise noted.

[6] CCC 405.

[7] Ibid.

[8] Cf. Leo F. Stelton, *Dictionary of Ecclesiastical Latin* (Peabody, MA: Hendrickson Publishers, 1995).

[9] CCC 2515.

[10] Cf. CCC 1264.

Concupiscence stems from the disobedience of the first sin. It unsettles man's moral faculties and, without being in itself an offense, inclines man to commit sins.[11]

The material effect of original sin known as concupiscence helps us understand our vulnerability to sensual lust — as well as our proclivity toward pride, greed, and envy. With regard to sex, all of these aspects can come into play. The man dominated by lust is often greedy, envious, and proud in his pursuit of sensual pleasure. Of course, lust is not the same as strong sexual desire, which, when controlled or ordered toward marital love and procreation can be something healthy and good. Lust is disordered sexual desire. It is craving for sexual pleasure beyond the proper order of spousal love. Satan is aware of our vulnerability to temptations of the flesh. The Evil One can introduce false and empty promises of happiness in this domain, and he likewise can prey upon our inclination toward envy if we think others are enjoying something we are not.

The sexual drive is directed by nature toward something good — an intimate, physical union between a man and a woman that can bring forth new human life. If the act by which we procreate were not desirable and attractive, the human race would die out. This natural drive, however, must be ruled by reason;[12] otherwise it can overwhelm us and become a destructive force.

In the history of the Christian literature, there is probably no more vivid description of the overwhelming power of sensual lust than the *Confessions* of St. Augustine (354–430). Born in North Africa to a pagan father and a Christian mother (St. Monica), Augustine relates how, as a 16-year-old student, he went to Carthage where in his ears "were the sizzling and frying of unholy loves."[13] As Augustine describes his state:

---

[11] CCC 2515.

[12] Cf. ibid.

[13] Augustine, *The Confessions*, book 3, 1; from, Rex Warner, trans. *The Confessions of St. Augustine* (New York and Scarborough, Ontario: New American Library, 1963), 52.

And so I muddied the clear spring of friendship with the dirt of physical desire and clouded over its brightness with the dark hell of lust.[14]

By age 17 or 18, Augustine began living with a woman. After about a year, she gave birth to their son, Adeodatus, or "gift of God." For about twelve more years, Augustine continued living with this woman as his mistress. During this time, he taught rhetoric — first in Carthage, then in Rome, and finally in Milan.

Augustine was a seeker of the truth, and he gradually moved from the dualistic religion of Manichaeism to Platonism and finally to Christ via the prayers of his mother, Monica, and the preaching of St. Ambrose, the bishop of Milan. When he became engaged to a young girl (at his mother's urging), Augustine separated from the mother of Adeodatus. He found, however, that he could not wait several years for his young fiancée to reach maturity. Instead, he took up with another mistress.

This state of affairs filled Augustine with self-reproach. He wanted to be chaste, but he recognized that he was not yet ready to be cured from "the disease of lust," which "preferred to be satisfied than extinguished."[15] Augustine saw his attachment to lust as slavery:

The enemy held my will and made a chain of it and bound me with it. From a perverse will came lust, and slavery to lust became a habit, and the habit, being constantly yielded to, became a necessity. These were like links, hanging each to each (which is why I call it a chain), and they held me fast in hard slavery.[16]

Augustine wanted to be free of this slavery to lust, but he realized that he was weak and needed God's power to liberate him. This, we can say, was a step in the right direction. He realized he was in bondage, and he cried out to God for help. As he writes:

---

[14] Ibid.
[15] Ibid., book 8, chap.7; Warner, 174.
[16] Ibid., book 8, chap.5; Warner, 168.

And you, Lord, in the secret places of my soul, stood above me in the severity of your mercy, redoubling the lashes of fear and shame, so that I should not give way once more and so that the weak piece of chain which still remained should not instead of snapping grow strong again and tie me down more firmly than before, and I was saying inside myself: "Now, now, let it be now!" and as I spoke the words I was already beginning to go in the direction I wanted to go. I nearly managed it, but I did not quite manage it. Yet I did not slip right back to the beginning. I was a state above that, and I stood there to regain my breath. And I tried again and I was very nearly there; I was almost touching it and grasping it, and then I was not there, I was not touching it, I was not grasping it.[17]

At this point, God intervened in a remarkable way. Augustine heard a singsong voice of a boy or a girl repeating the words: "Take it and read it. Take it and read it." He went to the book of the Apostle Paul, opened it, and read in silence the words of Romans 13:13–14: "Not in rioting and drunkenness, not in chambering and wantonness, not in strife and envying: but put ye on the Lord Jesus Christ, and make not provision for the flesh in concupiscence."[18] For Augustine, this was the turning point. As he tells us:

I had no wish to read further; there was no need to. For immediately I had reached the end of this sentence it was as though my heart was filled with a light of confidence and all the shadows of my doubt were swept away."[19]

Not long after this, Augustine and his son, Adeodatus, were baptized. The effect of the sacrament was profound; for, by being baptized, Augustine realized that "all anxiety for our past life vanished away."[20] Sadly, Adeodatus would die within a few years.

---

[17] Ibid., book 8, chap. 11; Warner, 180.
[18] As related in ibid., book 8, chap. 12; Warner, 183.
[19] Ibid.
[20] Ibid., book 9, chap. 6; Warner, 193.

Augustine, though, would go on to become a monk, a priest, a bishop, and one of the greatest theologians of the Catholic Church.

When I tell the story of Augustine's conversion to my students, some are surprised to learn that such a great saint of the Church struggled for many years with sexual lust. Yet his story is quite instructive. Augustine knew the power of lust, a power that can take over our wills and hold us in bondage. He likewise realized that only God's grace could free us from this bondage and give us serenity of heart, mind, and soul. It is not by accident that St. Augustine played such an important role in the formulation of the dogmas of original sin and the human dependence on the grace of Christ for salvation. These dogmas explain our vulnerability to sensual temptations and our reliance on divine assistance for liberation.

The *Catechism of the Catholic Church* describes chastity as "the successful integration of sexuality within the person and thus the inner unity of man in his bodily and spiritual being."[21] We likewise are told that "chastity lets us love with upright and undivided heart."[22] As a fruit of the Holy Spirit, chastity is a perfection formed in us by God.[23] Yet this perfection requires effort on our part and cooperation with God's grace. The struggle for chastity is part of the "spiritual battle" that we engage in as we strive to overcome the material effects of original sin in our lives.[24] But we are never alone in this struggle. Not only have others, like St. Augustine, struggled with concupiscence, but also God, in His mercy, offers us His love and grace to free us from the destructive impulses of the flesh.

Our secular culture gives the false impression that men and women who are sexually indulgent are happy and liberated. The story of St. Augustine reveals how deceptive such "happiness" is. Sexual "thrill-seeking" is chaotic, exploitive, and self-destructive. The Catholic understanding of sex is grounded in reality and not the "empty promises" of the Evil One. St. Paul speaks of the rebel-

---

[21] CCC 2337.
[22] CCC 2520.
[23] Cf. CCC 1832.
[24] Cf. CCC 405.

lion of the flesh against the spirit.[25] This does not mean that our bodily nature is bad. The "flesh" in this context refers to fallen human nature dominated by self-assertion and concupiscence. God's grace enlightens our minds and strengthens our wills so we may understand sexuality according to His design and exercise it accordingly. Because of original sin, sexuality, which is good and holy in its proper order, is subject to distortion and misuse. Without the grace that comes from the Holy Spirit, the "works of the flesh" will dominate our lives and not the fruit of the Spirit.[26]

If we believe in God, we should trust that His commandments are given for our own good. We should also trust His Church to guide us properly. The Catholic understanding of sexuality is not motivated by a puritanical distrust of pleasure. As will be seen in the subsequent chapters, Catholic sexual morality is rooted in Sacred Scripture and human reason. Rather than depriving human beings of happiness, it supports our call to beatitude in this world and the life to come.

---

[25] Cf. Gal 5:16–17, 24; Eph 2:3; CCC 2515.
[26] Cf. Gal 5:16–25.

CHAPTER TWO

IN THE BEGINNING:
THE THEOLOGY OF THE BODY

When I was teaching at a Catholic high school in the early 1980s, one of my students asked me, "If God wants us to abstain from sex until marriage, why did He give us such strong sexual urges?" The question this young man asked is one that I'm sure many others have also raised. I don't think anyone will deny that sexual abstinence before marriage is a challenge in today's sensually charged culture, and such a challenge can be an occasion for heroic virtue. The question, though, is whether sexual urges are simply appetites to be fulfilled. Is there a deeper meaning to human sexuality than the mere satisfaction of bodily desires?

Pope John Paul II explored the meaning of human sexuality more deeply than any other Roman Pontiff. Trained as a philosopher and a theologian, he lectured on the Catholic understanding of sexuality and marriage as a university professor and later as the Archbishop of Krakow, Poland. After his election as Pope in 1978, he was able to share his insights on the mystery of the human person with the whole Catholic world.

In a series of catechetical talks given between September 1979 and November 1984, John Paul II developed the main themes of what is now known as "the theology of the body." Going back to the first chapters of Genesis, the great Pontiff wished to understand God's plan for humanty's bodily existence as revealed "from the beginning" — the reference point taken by our Lord in Mt 19:4–6.

As John Paul II notes, Jesus refers to two key passages of Genesis. The first is that "he who made them from the beginning made them male and female" (Mt 19:4; cf. Gen 1:27). The second is that "therefore a man leaves his father and his mother and cleaves to his wife, and they become one flesh" (Gen 2:24; cf. Mt 19:5). To these two verses, Christ provides the normative conclusion: "What therefore, what God has joined together, no human being must separate" (Mt 19:6). John Paul sees this conclusion as crucial: "In light of these words of Christ, Genesis 2:24 sets forth the principle of the unity and indissolubility of marriage as the very content of the Word of God, expressed in the most ancient revelation."[1]

From this starting point, John Paul illuminates the key insights of Genesis 1–3. In Genesis 1:26–28, he locates three basic truths: (1) that God created man in His image and likeness; (2) that God created man as corporeal, as male and female; and (3) that God blesses man in his corporeal reality as male and female saying, "Be fruitful and multiply, and fill the earth and subdue it and have dominion over it" (Gen. 1:28).

John Paul II, though, focuses more on the truth about man revealed in Genesis 2, the second creation story. There, he finds the mystery of man in "original solitude." Man "finds himself alone before God mainly to express, through his first self-definition, his own self-knowledge as the original and fundamental manifestation of mankind."[2] Man realizes his original solitude because he knows he is different from "the whole world of living beings (*animalia*)."[3]

---

[1] John Paul II, General audience of September 5, 1979, in John Paul II, *The Theology of the Body: Human Love in the Divine Plan* [henceforth TOB] (Boston: Pauline Books & Media, 1997), 26. A new translation of John Paul II's Wednseday's audiences on the "theology of the body" has recently appeared with an outstanding introduction, viz. John Paul II, *Man and Woman He Created Them: A Theology of the Body,* trans. Michael Waldstein (Boston: Pauline Books & Media, 2006)[henceforth, Waldstein]. There is also a recent book by Marc Cardinal Ouellet of Québec that deeply enters into the Trinitarian dimensions of the "theology of the body," viz., *Divine Likeness: Toward a Trinitarian Anthropology of the Family,* trans. Philip Milligan and Linda Cicone (Grand Rapids, MI and Cambridge, UK: William B. Eerdmans Publishing Company, 2006).

[2] John Paul II, General audience of October 10, 1979; TOB, 37.

[3] Ibid.

Yet "it is not good that the man should be alone," and so God decides to create for him "a helper fit for him" (Gen 2:18). None of the other animals proves to be suitable, so God casts a deep sleep on the man, takes out one of his ribs and forms a woman, the suitable partner, for him (cf. Gen 2:21–22). The sleep, John Paul II suggests, "indicates a return to the moment preceding the creation, that through God's creative initiative, solitary 'man' may emerge from it again in his double unity as 'male and female.'"[4]

When God brings the woman to the man, the man exclaims: "This at last is bone of my bones and flesh of my flesh" (Gen 2:23). The discovery of his suitable partner moves the man from solitude to communion. This "communion of persons" (*communio personarum*) reveals man to be, in his own way, "an image of the inscrutable divine communion of persons."[5]

John Paul II finds in the human body, as male and female, the basis for "the mutual self-giving of the persons."[6] Prior to the fall, man and woman were not ashamed of their nakedness. This nakedness, according to the Pope, "signifies all the simplicity and fullness of the vision through which the 'pure' value of humanity as male and female, the 'pure' value of the body and of sex, is manifested."[7]

Within this context, the Pontiff highlights the "nuptial" or "spousal" meaning of the body.[8] The male body and the female body are designed to unite in love. This love, however, is one of self-donation. It is a love in which the husband and wife present their bodies as gifts to the other in full knowledge and freedom. This gift of love must be free in order for it to be a true gift. John Paul II links this freedom to the very meaning of human existence. As he observes:

> This freedom lies exactly at the basis of the spousal meaning of the body. The human body, with its sex — its masculinity and

---

[4] John Paul II, General audience of November 7, 1979; TOB, 44.
[5] John Paul II, General audience of November 14, 1979; TOB, 46.
[6] John Paul II, General audience of November 21, 1979; TOB, 50.
[7] John Paul II, General audience of January 2, 1980; TOB, 57.
[8] Waldstein translates *il significato "sponsale" del corpo* as the "spousal" meaning of the body, which seems preferable; see references in Waldstein, 682.

femininity — seen in the very mystery of creation, is not only a source of fruitfulness and of procreation, as in the whole natural order, but contains "from the beginning" the "spousal" attribute, that is, *the power to express love: precisely that love in which the human person becomes a gift* and — through this gift — fulfills the very meaning of his being and existence. We recall here the text of the most recent Council in which it declares that man is the only creature in the visible world that God willed "for its own sake," adding that this man cannot "fully find himself except through a sincere gift of self" [*Gaudium et Spes*, 24:3].[9]

For John Paul II, all of these themes come together: the nuptial meaning of the body; the communion of persons rooted in love; and this love as a free gift of the self in an act of self-donation. He goes on to apply these themes to the Catholic teaching on the regulation of birth. Pope Paul VI, in his 1968 encyclical, *Humanae Vitae*, had condemned contraception because of the "unbreakable connection between the unitive meaning and the procreative meaning [of the conjugal act]."[10] John Paul II deepens the understanding of this doctrine by applying the categories of the "theology of the body." What Paul VI taught chiefly by an appeal to "the natural law," John Paul II develops according to "a new personalist approach based on his philosophical work."[11]

At the heart of John Paul II's approach is the recognition of "the language of the body" manifested in "the very structure of the conjugal act as such."[12] His words on this subject are worthy of contemplation:

> The human body is not only the field of reactions of a sexual character, but it is at the same time the means of the expression of man as an integral whole, of the person, which reveals

---

[9] John Paul II, General audience of January 16, 1980; Waldstein, 185–186; cf. TOB, 63.

[10] Paul VI, *Humanae Vitae*, 12; Smith, Janet E., 281.

[11] John S. Grabowski, "Foreword" to TOB, 16.

[12] John Paul II, General audience of August 8, 1984; TOB, 395.

itself through the "language of the body." This "language" has an important interpersonal meaning, especially in the area of the reciprocal relations between man and woman.... As ministers of a sacrament that is constituted through consent and perfected by conjugal union, man and woman are called *to express* the mysterious "language" of their bodies in all the truth that properly belongs to it. Through gestures and reactions, through the whole reciprocally conditioned dynamism of tension and enjoyment — whose direct source is the body in its masculinity and femininity, the body in its action and interaction — through all this *man, the person*, "speaks."[13]

This is a very profound insight and one that is tragically ignored in many circles today. We speak with our bodies. In everyday life, we communicate by hand gestures, facial expressions, hugs, kisses, handshakes, etc. What, then, is communicated by the conjugal act? John Paul II offers these insights:

... [T]he conjugal act "means" not only love, but also potential fruitfulness, and thus it cannot be deprived of its full and adequate meaning by means of artificial interventions. In the conjugal act, it is not licit to separate artificially the unitive meaning from the procreative meaning, because the one as well as the other belong to the innermost truth of the conjugal act.... One can say that in the case of an artificial separation of these two meanings in the conjugal act, a real bodily union is brought about, but it does not correspond to the inner truth and dignity of personal communion, "*communio personarum.*" This communion demands, in fact, that the language of the body be expressed reciprocally in the integral truth of its meaning. If this truth is lacking, one can speak neither of the truth of the reciprocal gift of self nor of the reciprocal acceptance of oneself by the person. Such a violation of the

---

[13] John Paul II, General audience of August 22, 1984; Waldstein, 631–632; cf. TOB, 397–398.

inner order of conjugal communion, a communion that plunges its roots into the very order of the person, *constitutes the essential evil of the contraceptive act.*[14]

More will be said about the Catholic Church's teaching against contraception at later points in this book. The purpose of this chapter has been to present the major themes of John Paul II's theology of the body. This theology helps us understand the interpersonal dimension of human sexuality as grounded in God's creation of human beings as male and female. The biblical revelation is not simply an affirmation of the biological or physical dimensions of human sexuality and procreation. The theology of the body goes much deeper than that. The spousal meaning of the body shows that God created us as persons who are called to communion through self-donation. There is a special language of the body involved in the conjugal act that moves it beyond mere sensual gratification. The very nature of this act expresses a language of total, committed, and faithful love directed to the mysterious and wondrous power of procreation. This is the language God has written into the sexual act.

Because of original sin we have difficulty discerning the language of the body correctly. The reality of concupiscence often obscures our perception of the true meaning and purpose of sexual love. By His cross and resurrection, Christ has redeemed us from the power of sin, death, and the Devil. The grace of Christ imparted through the sacraments helps to heal our wounded nature and direct us back to God. In the next chapter, we will explore how the sacrament of marriage participates in the redemptive work of Christ and how the grace of this sacrament cooperates with the plan of God for our salvation.

---

[14] Ibid., Waldstein, 632–633; cf. TOB, 398.

CHAPTER THREE

THE BEAUTY, HOLINESS, AND INDISSOLUBILITY OF MARRIAGE

It's been a long time since I've been to a bachelor's party. This is probably because my male friends are either married or are priests. In any case, I've often wondered what is the purpose of these parties. I can certainly understand why friends of a prospective groom might wish to arrange such a gathering. When a man gets married, his whole life changes. He must plan his recreation time with his wife in mind, and he's not as free to socialize with male friends. When a bachelor party is held as a gesture of affection for a friend whose life is soon to change, it is a noble and worthy event.

The bachelor parties that puzzle me are those that get naughty and raucous. I've heard stories of heavy drinking, wild music, and "exotic" female dancers. I even heard a story about a man who took up with a "lady" of questionable morals the night before his scheduled wedding. His fiancée paid a surprise visit to his apartment only to find him sexually involved with this woman. Needless to say, the wedding was cancelled and there was much upset, but the prospective bride was spared getting married to a man who did not really love her.

What, though, is the purpose of a bachelor[1] party that takes the form of a Dionysian festival or Bacchanalia[2]? One explanation

---

[1] I've heard that there are also "bachelorette" parties, but I don't know enough about these to comment.

[2] Dionysius was the ancient Greek god of wine and frenzy. His Latin counterpart was Bacchus from whom the word Bacchanalia (drunken feast) is derived.

is that the groom is leaving behind a life of sexual license, and his friends wish to provide him one last night of "liberation" before he becomes a "one-woman" man. A more benevolent interpretation would be that marriage is a "rite of passage" from the uncommitted life of a bachelor to the committed life of a husband and potential father. The friends of the groom wish to celebrate the good times he enjoyed with them before he goes off into his new life.

Getting married is certainly a "rite of passage," but it's much more. It is a sacrament, a holy mystery, "an efficacious sign, instituted by Christ and entrusted to the Church, by which divine life is entrusted to us."[3] One of the most beautiful prayers in the "Rite of Marriage" is the nuptial blessing given by the priest that says:

> Father, you have made the union of man and wife so holy a mystery that it symbolizes the marriage of Christ and his Church.
>
> Father, by your plan man and woman are united, and married life has been established as the one blessing that was not forfeited by original sin or washed away by the flood.[4]

Marriage is a sacred mystery that symbolizes the covenantal love between Christ and His Church (cf. Eph 5:21–32). It is a primordial blessing that goes back to the creation of the human race. The dynamics of this blessing should be obvious: love, intimacy, communion, and fruitfulness. So precious are these gifts that God preserved them for humanity even after the fall.

Marriage and Sexuality in Scripture and Tradition

We have already discussed the fundamental teachings on marriage provided in Sacred Scripture, especially in Gen 1–2. God wills man and woman to unite as one flesh and to be fruitful and multiply. Our Lord, though, makes clear that the husband and wife are

---

[3] CCC 1131.

[4] Taken from Fr. Joseph R. Giandurco and Fr. John S. Bonnici, *Partners in Life and Love: A Preparation Handbook for the Celebration of Catholic Marriage* (New York: Alba House, 2002), 80.

joined together by God and, therefore, their union is indissoluble (cf. Mt 19:4–6).

In the Old Testament, the "divine pedagogy" on marriage is not yet complete, though there are some wonderful testimonies of marital love and fidelity in the books of Ruth, Tobit, and Song of Solomon.[5] Nevertheless, because of the Israelites' "hardness of heart" (Mt 19:8), Moses allowed men to divorce their wives (cf. Deut 24:1). God also tolerated polygamy during the time of the patriarchs and the kings, but Christ explicitly ruled out this practice (cf. Mt 19:3–9; Mk 10:1–12; Lk 16:18). Commenting on Mt 19:5, Pope Innocent III in 1201 writes that Scripture "does not say 'three or more,' but 'two;' nor did it say: 'he will cling to wives,' but to [his] 'wife.'"[6]

The New Testament's affirmation of the holiness and indissolubility of marriage continued in the early Church. Patristic writers such as St. Irenaeus (c. 130–200) and Clement of Alexandria (c. 150–215) were forced to defend the sanctity of marriage against certain Gnostic groups, which considered sex, marriage and procreation as evil.[7] The Church Fathers also had to uphold the holiness of sex — and its natural connection to marriage, and procreation — in the midst of the sexual license prevalent in the ancient Greco-Roman world.[8]

For the most part, the Fathers saw procreation as the primary justification for sexual union in marriage, but some, like Lactantius (c. 240–320) and St. John Chrysostom (c. 347–407), also believed it could be permitted as a means for avoiding concupiscence.[9]

St. Augustine (354–430) is probably the Church Father who has had the greatest influence on the theology of marriage. This is especially true with respect to his articulation of the three goods

---

[5] Cf. CCC 1611.

[6] Denz.-H, 778; the Council of Trent solemnly condemns polygamy for Christians in Denz.-H, 1802.

[7] Lawler et al., 47–50.

[8] Ibid.

[9] Ibid., 50; this teaching was derived from 1 Cor 7:9.

(*bona*) of marriage: offspring (*proles*), fidelity (*fides*), and sacrament (*sacramentum*).[10]

In its "Decree for the Armenians," the Council of Florence articulates the three goods of marriage as follows:

> The first is the accepting of children and educating them for the worship of God; the second is fidelity, which each of the spouses must observe with respect to the other; the third is the indissolubility of marriage, because it signifies the invisible union of Christ and the Church.[11]

Clearly, this is an adaptation of Augustine's three goods, with the sacrament expressed by reference to its indissolubility (*indivisibilitas*). The three goods of marriage are later elaborated on by Pius XI in his 1930 encyclical, *Casti Connubii*, with explicit reference to Augustine.[12] Like the Council of Florence, Pius XI also understands the good of "sacrament" as "the indissolubility of the matrimonial bond and the elevation and consecration of this contract by Christ into an efficacious sign of grace."[13]

Because marriage has offspring as one of its principal goods, sexual union is understood as a positive good. Augustine is sometimes criticized for believing all sexual pleasure is sinful, even in marriage. This, though, is not accurate. He understood that sexual union couldn't take place "without carnal pleasure, which, however, when moderated and used naturally, cannot be the same as concupiscence."[14]

The carnal pleasure that accompanies marital intercourse properly pursued is not sinful at all. Augustine, however, believed venial sin

---

[10] Augustine, *De bono conjugali*, 24, n. 32 as cited in Denz.-H, 3703. In addition to these three main goods, Augustine also saw other benefits to marriage such as serving as a "remedy for sensuality" and supporting the "relationship of love between the husband and wife;" see Augustine, *The Excellence of Marriage*, 6 [*De bono conjugali*], trans. Ray Kearney. *The Works of St. Augustine Part I Vol. 9: Marriage and Virginity*, ed. John E. Rotelle, O.S.A. (Hyde Park, NY: New City Press, 1997), 34–38.

[11] Denz.-H, 1327.

[12] Denz.-H, 3703–3714.

[13] Denz.-H, 3710.

[14] Augustine, *De bono conjugali*, c. 16, no. 18, as cited in Lawler et al., 268.

would be present if one of the spouses engaged in marital intercourse *only* for pleasure or *only* as a means of resisting fornication.[15] He also thought that a husband should not seek sexual intercourse from his wife if she was already pregnant, since a child could not be conceived.[16] If the spouses engaged in marital relations knowing that they were sterile, mortal sin would not be involved; venial sin, though, could be present.[17] Augustine understood that marriage could serve as a "remedy for sensuality."[18] Therefore, if marital intercourse "is for the purpose of satisfying sensuality, but still with one's spouse, because there is marital fidelity, it is a venial sin."[19] Because adultery and fornication involve mortal sin, it is far better to satisfy sensuality with one's spouse in order to avoid the consequences of mortal sin.

The *Poenitentiales* (or early medieval handbooks of penance) were heavily influenced by Augustine, but they tended to be even more severe. Not only did many of these penitential books require complete continence in the case of barrenness, but they also demanded abstinence from marital relations "during certain seasons of the year, on holy days, and prior to receiving communion."[20]

These penitential books represented the opinion of certain schools of thought and not the universal Church, but they were nonetheless influential. Later medieval theologians tended to follow more closely the ideas of Augustine himself. Thus, St. Albert the Great (1200–1280), like Augustine, accepted the goodness of marital intercourse for the purpose of procreation, but he believed venial sin would be present if intercourse were engaged in during pregnancy and when there was known sterility.[21]

---

[15] Cf. Lawler et al., 53–54. It should be noted that the venial sin would only be on the part of the spouse who sought intercourse for these reasons.

[16] Augustine, *De Bono Conjugali*, chapters 5–6; cf. John C. Ford, S.J., and Gerald Kelly, S.J., *Contemporary Moral Theology, Volume II: Marriage Questions* (Westminster, MD: The Newman Press, 1963), 173.

[17] Ford and Kelly, 174.

[18] Augustine, *The Excellence of Marriage*, 6 in *The Works of St. Augustine, Part I, Vol. 9: Marriage and Virginity*, 37.

[19] Ibid., 37–38.

[20] Lawler et al., 56; cf. also Ford and Kelly, 175–177.

[21] Ford and Kelly, 177. Apparently one reason St. Albert thought intercourse during pregnancy was a venial sin was because it could lead to an abortion.

St. Bonaventure (c. 1217–1274) and St. Thomas Aquinas (c. 1225–1274), however, went beyond Augustine by maintaining, "that the spouses could rightly choose to unite in marital coition in order to foster and express the good of fidelity."[22] Although they often spoke of the marital act as one of justice or duty, there were times when these two saints spoke of the union as an expression of love or friendship.[23] St. Thomas had a realistic view of the pleasure of the marital act, and he accepted this pleasure as a positive good associated with a morally good act.[24] On the other hand, he believed marital intercourse would be sinful if pursued *only* for the purpose of pleasure and not for other goods such as procreation, fidelity, or spousal friendship. In this, he was expressing the common teaching of the Church, which reappears in Pope Innocent XI's 1679 censure of the following laxist thesis:

> The conjugal act exercised only for pleasure is completely devoid of all fault and venial defect (*Opus coniugii ob solam voluptatem exercitum omni penitus caret culpa ac defectu veniali*).[25]

This, of course, does not mean that the pleasure, which accompanies marital intercourse, is sinful. It does, however, mean that — even in marriage — the spouses should avoid reducing each other to objects for the enjoyment of carnal pleasure. This is why John Paul II, in commenting on Mt 5:27–28, stated that: "Man can commit this adultery in the heart also with his own wife, if he treats her only as an object to satisfy instinct."[26]

---

[22] Lawler et al., 61.

[23] Ibid., 61–62 and 271. Cf. Aquinas, *Summa Contra Gentiles*, book 3, chap. 123, where he speaks of the love between husband and wife as the highest friendship (*maxima amicitia*), which is expressed not only in the marital act but "in the partnership of the entire domestic life" (*ad totius domesticae conversationis consortium*).

[24] Lawler et al., 63; cf. Aquinas's *Summa Theologica*, I–II, q. 31, a. 1–2; q. 33, a. 4 and q. 34, a. 4, for a discussion of the morality and propriety of pleasure. For more on Aquinas's appreciation of spousal love and pleasure in marriage, see Fabian Parmisano, OP, "Love and Marriage in the Middle Ages II," *New Blackfriars*, Vol. 50, No. 592 (September 1969): 649–66. On p. 655, Parmisano shows that Aquinas thought it madness (*insaniam*) to maintain that the act of marriage is always sinful; cf. *Summa Theologica*, suppl., 41, 3).

[25] Denz.-H, 2109.

[26] John Paul II, General audience of October 8, 1980; TOB, 157.

The French bishop, philosopher, and scientist Nicole Oresme (1323–1382) further developed the understanding of the marital act as an expression of spousal love. He saw the bond between husband and wife as "grounded upon love — a love that is productive of an intensity of joy and pleasure."[27] Thus, "the marriage act is good if decently and lovingly engaged in," and it has "purposes beyond generation."[28] Bishop Oresme's recognition of the beauty and goodness of spousal love anticipates in many ways the teaching of the Church's Magisterium, especially that of Vatican II's *Gaudium et Spes*, 48–51.

The Council of Trent (1545–1563) took up the doctrine of marriage in its 24th session (1563). Most notably, it reaffirmed the sacramentality and indissolubility of marriage in opposition to various Protestant opinions.[29] Although a complete theology of matrimony is not provided, some important points are made: marriage is a true sacrament instituted by Christ;[30] marriage must be monogamous;[31] Christian marriage is indissoluble and cannot be dissolved by heresy, distressing cohabitation, desertion, or adultery on the part of one of the spouses;[32] the Church has the authority to establish disqualifying impediments to marriage, reasons for separation from bed and board and other matters pertaining to the sacrament;[33] the married state does not surpass the state of virginity and celibacy, and it is better for those in this state to remain as virgins and celibates than to marry (cf. Mt 19:11f and 1 Cor 7:25f, 38 and 40).[34]

---

[27] Lawler et al., 66.

[28] Ibid.

[29] The dignity of marriage as a sacrament had been previously recognized by Pope Lucius III at the Council of Verona in 1185 (Denz.-H, 761); by the Profession of Faith of Emperor Michael Palaeologus read at the Second Council of Lyons in 1274 (Denz.-H, 860); by Pope John XXII in his constitution, *Gloriosam Ecclesiam*, of 1318 (Denz.-H, 916); and several times by the Council of Florence in 1439 (Denz.-H, 1310 and 1327). There are also strong scriptural and patristic supports for marriage as a sacrament.

[30] Denz.-H, 1800–1801.

[31] Denz.-H, 1798, 1802.

[32] Denz.-H, 1797, 1805, 1807.

[33] Denz.-H, 1803–1804; 1808–1809; 1811–1812.

[34] Denz.-H, 1810.

The Council of Trent also issued a number of disciplinary canons for the reform of marriage in its decree known as *Tamesti*. The ten canons issued concern such matters as clandestine marriages (canon 1); spiritual relations (canon 2); consanguinity (canon 5); abduction (canon 6); concubinage (canon 8); coerced marriages (canon 9); and the prohibition of solemn celebrations of marriage during Advent, Christmas, Lent, and Easter (canon 10).[35]

The basic teachings of Trent on marriage were incorporated in the 1566 *Catechism of the Council of Trent* (also known as the *Roman Catechism*). With regard to the conjugal act, wives are advised to yield to their husbands "in all things not inconsistent with Christian piety" (*quae Christianae pietati non adversantur*).[36] The Roman Catechism likewise observes that "marriage is not to be used for purposes of lust or sensuality," and St. Jerome is cited counseling husbands to love their wives "with judgment" not "indulgence" for "there is nothing more shameful than that a husband should love his wife as an adulteress."[37] The faithful, following 1 Cor. 7:5, are also encouraged to abstain from the conjugal act at various times to devote themselves to prayer. Such abstinence "is particularly to be observed for at least three days before Communion, and oftener during the solemn fast of Lent."[38]

In the post-Tridentine era, the Jesuit Tomás Sanchez (1550–1610) provided a thorough treatment of the major theological and moral issues concerning matrimony in his three-volume, ten-book treatise, *Disputationum de sancto matrimonii sacramento*,

---

[35] A portion of *Tamesti* can be found in Denz.-H, 1813–1816; the complete text can be found in *The Decrees of the Ecumenical Councils, Volume II (Trent-Vatican II)*, ed. Norman P. Tanner, S.J., (London and Washington, DC: Sheed & Ward and Georgetown University Press, 1990), 755–759.

[36] *Catechismus ex Decreto SS Concilii Tridentini ad Parochos* [*Catech. Rom.*] part II, chap. VIII, n. 27; cf. *The Catechism of the Council of Trent* [the *Roman Catechism*], trans. John A McHugh, O.P., and Charles J. Callan, O.P. (Rockford, IL: Tan Books and Publishers, 1982), 352.

[37] *Catech. Rom.*, part II, chap. VIII, n. 33; *The Catechism of the Council of Trent*, trans. McHugh and Callan, 355; cf. Jerome, *Contra Iovian*, book 1.

[38] *Catech. Rom.*, part II, chap. VIII, n 34; *The Catechism of the Council of Trent*, trans. McHugh and Callan, 355.

usually referred to as *De Matrimonio* (1602 and 1605).[39] Sanchez discussed the question of the motives needed for the marital act to be moral. He was less stringent than some of his predecessors. He did not believe it was always necessary to have an explicit intent of the "honest ends of marriage" (procreation, the fostering of fidelity, etc.) for conjugal union to be licit. Rather, it was only necessary that the spouses intend conjugal union "as spouses" and that the basic ends of marriage are respected.[40] Sanchez's Jesuit contemporary, Aegidius de Coninck (1571–1633) supported this position, as did the School of Salamanca and St. Alphonsus Liguori (1696–1787).[41] By the nineteenth century, this became the standard opinion of Catholic moralists.[42] The spouses only need a habitual intent of the proper ends of the marital act; and such intent need not be explicit in every instance of conjugal union.[43]

The Characteristics of Marital Love

St. Augustine supplied the Catholic Church with a clear articulation of the three goods (*bona*) of marriage: offspring, fidelity, and sacrament. As we have already seen, these three goods became standard for the Catholic theology of marriage.[44] Men and women, of course, get married because they love each other, but the type of love required is not partial or temporary; it is total. The special type of love involved in marriage is called "conjugal love," because this love unites or joins together the spouses both physically and spiritually.

Pope Paul VI, in his 1968 encyclical, *Humanae Vitae*, described the four main characteristics of conjugal love as: (1) fully human;

---

[39] Cf. R. Brouillard, "Sanchez, Thomas" in *Dictionnaire de Théologie Catholique*, Vol. 14, p. 1 (Paris: Libraire Letouzey et Ané, 1939), 1075–1085.

[40] Cf. Ford and Kelly, 180, and Lawler et al., 66.

[41] Cf. Lawler et al., 66–67, and Ford and Kelly, 180–182.

[42] Lawler et al., 66–67.

[43] Ibid.

[44] In addition to the Magisterial documents already cited, these three ends are found in the *Catechism of the Council of Trent*; cf. *Catechismus Ex Decreto SS. Concilii Tidentini*, pars. II, cap. VIII, n. 23.

(2) total; (3) faithful and exclusive; and (4) fruitful.[45] These four characteristics need to be considered carefully.

The first characteristic of married love is that it is *fully human*. It is not merely an instinct or "an emotional drive." Rather it involves "an act of the free will," something that expresses the human dignity of husband and wife as free and rational beings. By their free gift of themselves to each other, they establish that trust, which "is meant to survive the joys and sorrows of daily life." This trust enables them "to grow, so that husband and wife become in a way one heart and one soul, and together attain their human fulfillment" (no. 9).

Married love is also *total*; it is a "very special form of friendship in which husband and wife generously share everything, allowing no unreasonable exceptions and not thinking solely of their own convenience" (no. 9). The husband and wife are caught up in a total love that moves beyond a consideration of what they each receive. This love cherishes the other for his or her own sake, and it involves a mutual giving by which each spouse becomes a "gift" to the other.

Married love is likewise "*faithful and exclusive* of all other, and this until death" (no. 9). Because they freely vowed themselves to each other, fidelity and exclusivity are necessary expressions of authentic marital love. This mutual fidelity is, at times, difficult, but it is always "honorable and meritorious," and a "source of profound and enduring happiness" (no. 9).

Finally, married love is *fruitful*, that is, directed toward procreation. Citing the pastoral constitution of Vatican II, *Gaudium et Spes*, Paul VI reaffirms that "marriage and conjugal love are by their nature ordered toward the procreation and education of children," and "children are really the supreme gift of marriage and contribute in the highest degree to their parents' welfare" (no. 9; cf. *Gaudium et Spes*, 50).

---

[45] Paul VI, *Humanae Vitae*, 9; see Janet E. Smith *Humanae Vitae: A Challenge to Love* (New Hope, KY: New Hope Publications, nd), 29–30.

Men and women might get married for a variety of reasons. Sometimes, they are lonely and seeking companionship. Sometimes, they have strong sexual desires and marriage provides an honorable way of channeling these desires. Sometimes, they are seeking stability and mutual assistance. In other cases, they are actually looking for someone to help them grow in holiness. Whatever motivates people to get married (and often it's a combination of motivations), they cannot change the authentic characteristics of conjugal love. Appendix A discusses the more technical aspects of the "essential ends and properties of marriage." For now, the question of the indissolubility of marriage needs to be examined in more depth.

The Indissolubility of Marriage

The Catholic Church teaches that a true, sacramental marriage is indissoluble.[46] Only the death of one of the spouses would permit another marriage to take place. Many people, including Catholics, find this teaching difficult to accept. Why should a man and a woman continue in a marriage that has failed? Should not divorced Catholics have the right to marry again? Should not the Church show greater compassion in this regard?

The Church's response to such questions is one of authentic compassion. The indissolubility of marriage supports the good of all the parties involved: the husband, the wife, the children, and the common good of society. What *Gaudium et Spes* 48 teaches on this deserves repeating: "The intimate union of marriage, as a mutual giving of two persons, and the good of the children demand total fidelity from the spouses and require an unbreakable unity between them." The indissolubility of marriage, therefore, is not an arbitrary imposition on human relations. Instead, it is a natural corollary of the intimate love that unites a man and a woman in marriage, a love that, by nature, is open to procreation. The indissolubility of marriage is also a sign of the restoration of the

---

[46] Cf. CCC 1614.

marital covenant to the "original order of creation" before it was "disturbed by sin."[47] In this respect, marriage is elevated to the dignity of a sacrament that reflects Christ's own covenantal love for His bride, the Church.[48]

While many reasons can be given in support of the indissolubility of marriage, the following deserve special attention: (1) The sexual act itself is an expression of complete self-giving that requires fidelity and indissolubility; (2) the indissolubility of marriage provides the proper support for the procreation and education of children and the common good of society; (3) the indissolubility of marriage is upheld in Scripture; and (4) the indissolubility of marriage is infallibly taught by the Church's Magisterium. As noted earlier, the Catholic understanding of sexual intimacy transcends the pursuit of mere erotic pleasure. Indeed, Vatican II teaches that marital love brings "together the human and the divine" and "leads the partners to a free and mutual giving of self."[49] The acts of sexual union within marriage are "noble and honorable," and they foster "the self-giving they signify."[50] As we have seen, Paul VI, in his 1968 encyclical *Humanae Vitae*, summarizes the chief characteristics of conjugal love as: (1) human (*humanus*); (2) total (*pleno*); (3) faithful and exclusive (*fidelis et exclusorius*); and (4) fruitful (*fecundus*).[51]

All four of these characteristics of conjugal love are interconnected. Because this love is human, it corresponds to the love between persons and not a mere biological or erotic act. Because conjugal love is total, it cannot be conditional or fleeting. Moreover, total love must be faithful and exclusive. This is why polygamy and adultery violate the Christian understanding of marital love.[52] Finally, since married love is truly human and total, it reaches beyond

---

[47] CCC 1615.
[48] Cf. Eph 5:25–26, 31–32 and CCC 1615–1666.
[49] *Gaudium et Spes*, 49.
[50] Ibid.
[51] Cf. Paul VI, *Humanae Vitae*, 9; see also Denz.-H, 4470–4473.
[52] Cf. CCC 1645 (on polygamy) and 2380 (on adultery).

the communion of the spouses "and seeks to raise up new lives."[53] God Himself has chosen to link conjugal love to procreation and human fruitfulness because He knows that children need the warmth and security that is best supplied by a mother and father united in the faithful, exclusive, and indissoluble covenant of marriage.

Because the sexual act is potentially life-giving, it requires the stability of faithful and committed love. There is something powerful, beautiful, and mysterious in the love that unites a man and a woman in marriage. As Pope Benedict XVI notes, amid all the multiple meanings of love, "one in particular stands out: love between man and woman, where body and soul are inseparably joined and human beings glimpse an apparently irresistible promise of happiness."[54] Sexual union is only properly understood as marital union, and marital love, by its very nature, is total, faithful, exclusive, and fruitful.

To engage in sexual intercourse outside of marriage always involves an element of dishonesty. In this context, a man and a woman unite in the act by which "they become one flesh" (Gen 2:24; Mt 19:5–6), but they are not truly one because their love lacks the totality and fidelity of the marital bond. Sexual intercourse symbolizes and embodies a union that is total, exclusive, and open to new life. Sexual union outside of marriage can only mimic these qualities of true love, because it always falls short of the reality itself. Written into the very language of conjugal union are the totality, exclusivity, and indissolubility of true marriage.

The natural link of sexual intercourse to procreation is another reason why marriage must be indissoluble. Because "marriage and married love are by nature ordered to the procreation and education of children,"[55] the indissolubility of marriage follows as a necessary support for the raising of children. Although the Church

---

[53] *Humanae Vitae*, 9; trans. Janet E. Smith, *Humanae Vitae: A Generation Later*, 279.

[54] Benedict XVI, *Deus Caritas Est*, 2.

[55] *Gaudium et Spes*, 50.

acknowledges that there are situations that might justify the "physical separation of the couple,"[56] divorce is always looked upon as a tragedy and a source of suffering. Pope Leo XIII, in his 1880 encyclical, *Arcanum Divinae Sapientiae*, described in vivid language the harms that come from divorce:

> Truly, it is hardly possible to describe how great are the evils that flow from divorce. Matrimonial contracts are by it made variable; mutual kindness is weakened; deplorable inducements to unfaithfulness are supplied; harm is done to the education and training of children; occasion is afforded for the breaking up of homes; the seeds of dissension are sown among families; the dignity of womanhood is lessened and brought low, and women run the risk of being deserted after having ministered to the pleasures of men.[57]

What Leo XIII taught in 1880 has been reiterated numerous times by the Magisterium. Not only does divorce contradict the divine and natural law,[58] it is also a source of grave harm to children.[59] Pius XII, in his 1942 "Allocution to Newlyweds," underscored the Church's concern for children who depend upon their parents for "being, nourishment, and upbringing."[60] The "harmonious formation and education" of children "are inconceivable without the undoubted fidelity of the parents."[61] Pius XII speaks of "the rupture" of this bond of fidelity as,

> ... cruelty toward [children] and contempt for their blood, a humiliating of their name, a division of their heart, and a sep-

---

[56] CCC 1649; cf. CIC, canons 1151–1151 and the Council of Trent's *Doctrine on the Sacrament of Marriage*, can. 8: Denz-H, 1808.

[57] Leo XIII, *Arcanum Divinae Sapientiae*, 29; *Matrimony: Papal Teachings*, no. 179, p.155.

[58] Cf. CCC 2384.

[59] See Patrick F. Fagan and Robert E. Rector, "The Effects of Divorce on America," http://www.heritage.org/research/family/BG1373.cfm. The authors point to higher rates of crime, drug abuse, poverty, and suicide among children of divorced parents as well as poorer grades in school.

[60] Pius XII, "Allocution to Newlyweds," in *Matrimony: Papal Teachings*, no. 497, p. 351.

[61] Ibid.

aration of brothers and home, a bitterness for their youthful happiness, and what is worse still, moral scandal. How many are the wounds to the souls of millions of youth? In many cases, what sad and lamentable ruin! What implacable remorse is planted in souls! The Church and civil society place their hopes in spiritually upright, morally pure, happy, and joyful men, who for the most part do not come from homes torn with discord and uncertain affection, but from those families wherein all is based on the fear of God and inviolate married fidelity.[62]

What the Pope observed in 1942 has become only more painfully true in the decades that have followed. This is why the *Catechism of the Catholic Church* speaks of divorce as "a grave offense against the natural law."[63] Divorce is likewise immoral "because it introduces disorder into the family and society" that "brings grave harm to the deserted spouse, to children traumatized by the separation of their parents and often torn between them."[64] The harm that is done to children through divorce has a "contagious effect, which makes it truly a plague on society."[65]

By upholding the indissolubility of marriage, the Catholic Church contributes to the common good of society. As John Paul II taught: "To bear witness to the inestimable value of the indissolubility and fidelity of marriage is one of the most precious and most urgent tasks of Christian couples in our time."[66] The same Pontiff also recognized that the indissolubility of marriage concerns "one of the cornerstones of society," and he believed efforts should be made to obtain "the public recognition of indissoluble marriage in the civil juridical order."[67]

---

[62] Ibid.

[63] CCC 2384.

[64] Ibid., 2385.

[65] Ibid.

[66] John Paul II, Apostolic Exhortation, *Familiaris Consortio*, 20: AAS 74 (1982), 104.

[67] John Paul II, Address to the Prelate Auditors, Official and Advocates of the Tribunal of the Roman Rota, Jan. 28, 2002, no .9; cf. John Paul II, *Letter to Families*, Feb. 2, 1994, no. 17.

In a similar manner, the Church has condemned efforts to make "de facto unions" the legal equivalent of marriage and various efforts to provide legal recognition to unions between homosexual persons.[68] Marriage between a man and a woman cannot be considered "just one possible form of marriage."[69] To do so would be a "grave detriment to the common good."[70] From the viewpoint of the Catholic Church, "the solidity of the family nucleus is a decisive force for the quality of life in society, therefore the civil community cannot remain indifferent to the destabilizing tendencies that threaten its foundations at their very roots."[71]

To be sure, the Catholic Church manifests pastoral love toward divorced people. Pastoral care, however, must be rooted in the divine and natural law. Otherwise, it will ultimately lead to harm for all concerned. The doctrine that sexual intimacy demands the security of an indissoluble union between a man and a woman is rooted in right reason or the natural law. We need only recall the harm done to individuals, especially children, when the stability of marriage is threatened. This is why the Church teaches that:

> By its very nature, conjugal love requires the inviolable fidelity of the spouses. This is a consequence of the gift of themselves, which they make to each other. Love seeks to be definitive; it cannot be an arrangement "until further notice." The "intimate union of marriage, as a mutual giving of two persons, and the good of the children, demand total fidelity from the spouses and require an unbreakable union between them."[72]

The indissolubility of marriage is a teaching found in Scripture and constantly upheld by the Magisterium of the Catholic

---

[68] Cf. Pontifical Council for Justice and Peace, *Compendium of the Social Doctrine of the Catholic Church* [henceforth, CSDC](USCCB Publishing, 2005), nos. 227–228, pp. 102–103; cf. also, Congregation for the Doctrine of the Faith, *Considerations regarding Proposals to Give Legal Recognition to Unions between Homosexual Persons*, June 3, 2003 [henceforth, CDF, *Considerations*, 2003].

[69] CSDC, no. 228, p. 103. Cf. CDF, *Considerations*, 2003, no. 8.

[70] CDF, *Considerations*, 2003, no. 8.

[71] CSDC, no. 229, p. 104.

[72] CCC 1646; cf. *Gaudium et Spes*, 48.

Church.[73] Moses permitted divorce because of the "hardness" of the hearts of those he taught,[74] but the "Lord Jesus insisted on the original intention of the Creator who willed that marriage be indissoluble."[75] In Mk 10:11, Jesus tells His disciples: "Whoever divorces his wife and marries another, commits adultery against her; and if she divorces her husband and marries another, she commits adultery." This teaching is repeated in Lk 16:18, where Jesus states that, "every one who divorces his wife and marries another commits adultery, and he who marries a woman divorced from her husband commits adultery." St. Paul makes it clear in 1 Cor 7:10–11 that he is handing on what the Lord taught, that "the wife should not separate from her husband (but if she does, let her remain single or else be reconciled to her husband) — and that the husband should not divorce his wife."

These Scriptures strongly support the indissolubility of marriage. But, if this is so, why do some Christian groups allow for divorce and remarriage? Some appeal to the "exceptive clauses" in Mt 5: 31 and 19:9 as evidence that the Church can grant exceptions to the general prohibition against divorce and remarriage. One Eastern Orthodox theologian, for example, cites Mt 19:9 in support of his Church's policy:

> The Orthodox Church permits divorce and remarriage, quoting as its authority, the text of Matthew 19:9, where our Lord says: 'if a man divorces his wife, *for any cause other than unchastity*, and marries another, he commits adultery.' Since Christ, according to the Matthaean account, allowed an exception to His general ruling about the indissolubility of marriage, the Orthodox Church also is willing to allow an exception. Certainly Orthodoxy regards the marriage bond as in principle lifelong and

---

[73] The witness of the Catholic Church to this truth so clearly taught by our Lord is a sign of her guidance by the Holy Spirit. It is not by accident that Churches and ecclesial communities that break from Catholic unity inevitably wind up compromising this teaching by their acceptance of divorce and remarriage.

[74] Mt 19:8.

[75] CCC 2382; cf. Mt 5:31–32; 19:3–9; Mk 10:9; Lk 16:18; 1 Cor 7:10–11.

indissoluble, and it sees the breakdown of marriage as a tragedy due to human weakness and sin. But while condemning the sin, the Church still desires to help suffering humans and allow them a second chance. When, therefore, a marriage has entirely ceased to be a reality, the Orthodox Church does not insist on the preservation of a legal fiction. Divorce is seen as an exceptional but necessary concession to human brokenness, living as we do in a fallen world. Yet, although assisting men and women to rise again after a fall, the Orthodox Church knows that a second alliance can never be the same as the first; and so in the service for a second marriage several of the joyful ceremonies are omitted, and replaced by penitential prayers. In practice, this second marriage service is scarcely ever used.

Orthodox Canon Law, while permitting a second or even a third marriage, absolutely forbids a fourth. In theory the canons only permit divorce in cases of adultery, but in practice it is granted for other reasons as well.[76]

At first glance, this seems eminently reasonable, but it fails to do justice to what Jesus actually teaches in the text. The exceptive clause in Mt 19:9 (and Mt 5:31–32) is for *porneia* (lewdness, incest, or sexual perversity) not *moicheia* (adultery). If adultery were included under the exception of *porneia*, then anyone wishing to divorce and marry again would only need to commit adultery to dissolve the marriage bond! This, though, would render void what Jesus teaches in the parallel texts of Mk 10:11–12 and Lk 16:18.

The Catholic Church understands the exception of *porneia* as referring to situations of sexual lewdness that render a "marriage" unlawful from the start.[77] The sexual lewdness here might pertain to cases of incest or consanguinity, or *porneia* might simply refer to

---

[76] Timothy Ware (Bishop Kallistos of Diokleia), *The Orthodox Church*, New Edition (London: Penguin Books, 1993), 295.

[77] The Revised New Testament of the New American Bible (1986) chooses to translate the exceptive clause in Mt 5:32 and 19:9 as "unless the marriage is unlawful." While this might not be a literal translation, it does communicate the sense of what is meant by the exception, i.e., some form of *porneia* (e.g., incest) that renders the marriage invalid from the start. On the Jewish background to Mt 5:32 and 19:9, see

fornication. In the latter case, a union that is really "fornication" is not lawful, and, therefore, it does not fall under the category of indissoluble marriage.[78]

In interpreting the New Testament, the Fathers of the Church "almost all expound the view that in the case of adultery the dismissal of the guilty party is permitted, but that a subsequent remarriage is forbidden."[79] The Protestant Reformers challenged marriage as a sacrament and questioned its indissolubility. By way of response, the Council of Trent, at its twenty-fourth session in 1563, solemnly upheld the sacramentality and indissolubility of marriage. The Council noted that the "perpetual and indissoluble bond of matrimony" was first pronounced by Adam and more clearly taught by Christ.[80] In Canon 1 of its "Doctrine of the Sacrament of Matrimony," Trent anathematized those who deny, "that matrimony is not truly and properly one of the seven sacraments of the Law of the Gospel instituted by Christ the Lord."[81] In Canon 5, those who say, "that the marriage bond can be dissolved because of heresy, or irksome cohabitation, or because of the willful desertion of one of the spouses,"[82] were likewise condemned. Canon 7 further anathematized those who say that

> ... the Church is in error for having taught and for still teaching that, in accordance with the evangelical and apostolic

---

Benedict T. Viviano, "The Gospel According to Matthew" in *The New Jerome Biblical Commentary*, ed. Raymond E. Brown et al. (Englewood Cliffs, NJ: Prentice Hall, 1990), no. 42:31-32, pp. 642-643, and Raymond F. Collins, *Divorce in the New Testament* (Collegeville, MN: The Liturgical Press, 1992): 184-213. With reference to Mt 5:32 and 19:9, the Council of Trent anathematized those who claim the Church errs in teaching that "the marriage bond cannot be dissolved because of adultery on the part of one of the spouses" (Denz. Hün, 1807).

[78] It should further be noted that the "Pauline Privilege" based on 1 Cor 7:12–15 in no way denies the indissolubility of marriages because it deals with the original union of two unbelievers rather than a sacramental marriage.

[79] Ludwig Ott, *The Fundamentals of Catholic Dogma,* trans. Patrick Lynch (St. Louis: B. Herder Book Company, 1958), 464.

[80] Denz.-H, 1797–1798.

[81] Denz.-H, 1801; trans. from *The Christian Faith in the Doctrinal Documents of the Catholic Church*, Revised Edition , eds. J. Neuner, S.J. and J. Dupuis, S.J. (New York: Alba House, 1982), no. 1808, p. 529.

[82] Denz.-H, 1805; Neuner and Dupuis, no. 1812, p. 529.

doctrine (cf. Mk 10; 1 Cor 7), the marriage bond cannot be dissolved because of adultery on the part of one of the spouses, and that neither of the two, not even the innocent one who has given no cause for infidelity, can contract another marriage during the lifetime of the other; and that the husband who dismisses an adulterous wife and marries again and the wife who dismisses an adulterous husband and marries again are both guilty of adultery.[83]

Because the ecumenical Council of Trent so clearly defines the indissolubility of marriage, this doctrine must be understood as an infallible teaching of the Catholic faith. Pope Pius VI, writing in 1789, further taught that even marriage in the state of nature, "long before it was raised to the dignity of a sacrament in the true sense of the word, was divinely instituted in such a manner that its bond was perpetual and indissoluble, so that it cannot be dissolved by any civil law."[84]

Separation, Divorce, and Annulments

While upholding the indissolubility of marriage, the Church recognizes that "there are some situations in which living together becomes impossible for a variety of reasons."[85] Even though the spouses live apart, they "do not cease to be husband and wife before God and so are not free to contract a new marriage."[86] If such separated spouses obtain civil divorces and enter into "new civil unions," the Church cannot accept these new unions as valid. Those who are divorced and are remarried civilly "find themselves in a situation that directly contravenes God's law," and, therefore, "they cannot receive Eucharistic communion as long as this situation persists."[87]

---

[83] Denz-H, 1807; Neuner and Dupuis, no. 1814, p. 529.

[84] Pius VI, Letter, *Litteris tuis*, July 11, 1789, to the Bishop of Agra; *Matrimony: Papal Teachings*, no. 48, p. 66.

[85] CCC 1649; cf. The Council of Trent acknowledgment of the possibility of temporary or indefinite "separation from bed and board" in Denz-H, 1808 and Neuner and Dupuis, no. 1815, p. 529.

[86] CCC 1650.

[87] Ibid.

Separated and divorced Catholics deserve "attentive solicitude, so that they do not consider themselves separated from the Church, in whose life they can and must participate as baptized persons."[88] When such Catholics live chastely and refuse to enter into a subsequent invalid union, they are to be commended for their heroic witness to the indissolubility of marriage.[89] With regard to divorced Catholics who have remarried, special care and prayer are needed. As noted above, they cannot be admitted to the Eucharist; and this is so not only because of their objective situation but also because their admittance to the Eucharist could lead to "confusion regarding the Church's teaching about the indissolubility of marriage."[90]

In many cases, separated or divorced Catholics should be encouraged to see if there might be grounds for a "declaration of nullity" with respect to their prior, putative marriages. Such declarations of nullity are popularly called "annulments," and even canon lawyers use this term. Properly speaking, though, the Church does not have the authority to annul a true, sacramental marriage. A marriage tribunal of the Catholic Church can, however, provide an official judgment "that what appeared to be a valid marriage was actually not one."[91] This is not a judgment that there was no love in the relationship, or that the people involved are bad Catholics. Instead, it is

a juridic determination that, at the time of the wedding, one or both parties to the marriage lacked sufficient *capacity* for marriage, or that one or both parties failed to give adequately their *consent* to marriage as the Church understands and proclaims it, or in weddings involving at least one Catholic, that the parties violated the Church's requirement of canonical *form* in getting married.[92]

---

[88] Ibid., 1651.

[89] Cf. John Paul II, *Familiaris Consortio*, 83.

[90] Ibid., 84.

[91] Edward Peters, J.D., J.C.D., *Annulments and the Catholic Church* (West Chester, PA: Ascension Press, 2004), 1. This book is highly recommended to all who have questions on this delicate subject.

[92] Ibid., 1–2 (emphasis in the original).

It is tragic that there are so many petitions for annulments in the United States. This does not necessarily mean that "U.S. tribunals are lax in their administration of justice."[93] It might, though, mean that many American Catholics enter into marriage poorly prepared and/or without proper capacity or consent. It must be emphasized, however, that a declaration of nullity is not equivalent to "Catholic divorce." A true, sacramental marriage is indissoluble. An annulment is simply a declaration by the Church that there never was a valid sacramental marriage to begin with. Clearly, much more needs to be done to assist engaged couples in understanding what the Catholic Church teaches about the indissolubility of marriage. In this way, there will be fewer cases of improper consent, fewer divorces, and fewer children enduring the wounds of broken homes.

---

[93] Ibid. in appendix, 170.

CHAPTER FOUR

SEXUAL SINS AND GOD'S MERCY

In Chapter One, we considered the case of the young St. Augustine as an example of how vulnerable we are to sexual lust because of original sin. Augustine's story likewise reminds us of our dependence on God's grace to heal us from lust and elevate us to chastity. In the chapters that follow, specific sexual sins will be considered: pornography (Chapter Five); masturbation (Chapter Six); homosexual acts (Chapter Seven); fornication and cohabitation (Chapter Eight); and offenses against marital chastity (Chapter Nine).

Before examining these specific types of sexual sin, we should reflect on sin in general and more specifically on sins of the flesh. How serious are sins of lust? Are they often linked to other sinful tendencies? Are there factors that can diminish culpability for such sins? These are some of the points that need to be considered, but more significantly, the topic of sin must never be separated from its necessary counterpart, God's mercy and forgiveness.

What does the Church mean by sin? The *Catechism of the Catholic Church* offers three basic definitions: (1) "Sin is an offense against reason, truth and right conscience;" (2) Sin "is failure in genuine love for God and neighbor caused by a perverse attachment to certain goods;" (3) Sin is "an utterance, a deed, or a desire contrary to the eternal law."[1] Sin is also variously described as "an offense against God" and "disobedience."[2]

---

[1] CCC 1849; for the third definition, cf. St. Augustine, *Contra Faustum* 22: PL 42, 418; St. Thomas Aquinas, *Summa Theologica* I–II, 71, 6.
[2] CCC 1850.

Scripture uses a number of words for sin. In the Old Testament, three Hebrew words are commonly used for sin: *hāttā'*, which means, "missing the mark; *pesha'*, which means rebellion; and *'awōn*, which means iniquity or guilt.[3] In Psalm 51:3–4, known as the *Miserere*," all three of these terms are used:

> Have mercy on me, O God, according to thy steadfast love; according to thy abundant mercy blot out my transgressions (*pesha'*). Wash me thoroughly from my iniquity (*'awōn*), and cleanse me from my sin (*hāttā't*)! For I know my transgressions (*pesha'*), and my sin (*hāttā't*) is ever before me. Against thee, thee only, have I sinned (*hāttā'*), and done that which is evil (*ra'*) in your sight.[4]

In the New Testament, the principal term for sin is *harmatia*. Thus, Jesus is described as the "Lamb of God, who takes away the sin (*harmatia[n]*) of the world,"[5] and He tells the paralytic: "My son, your sins (*hamartia[i]*) are forgiven" (Mk 2:5). The New Testament also employs other words related to sin such as lawlessness (*anomia*); darkness (*skotos*); and injustice (*adikia*).[6] Scripture not only recognizes the reality of sin, but it also teaches that certain sins can lead to spiritual death and exclusion from God's kingdom (cf. Deut 30:17; Mt 25: 41–46;1 Cor 6:9–10; Gal 5:19–21; Rev 21:8 and 22:15).

The Catholic Church distinguishes original sin from personal sin. The fall of Adam and Eve resulted in a human nature "deprived of original holiness and justice."[7] This inherited deprivation of holiness and grace has been variously described as a "stain" on the soul or an inborn "guilt." In reality, though, original sin "does not have the quality of a personal fault in any of Adam's

---

[3] Cf. William E. May, *An Introduction to Moral Theology*, Second Edition (Huntington, IN: Our Sunday Visitor, 2003), 186.

[4] Cf. Ibid., 186–187.

[5] Jn 1:29. Here the reference is to the "sin" of the world, but in the *Agnus Dei* of the Mass, Jesus is invoked as the "Lamb of God who takes away the sins (*peccata*) of the world." The "sin of the world" can be understood as original sin that Jesus takes away at baptism. But it's equally true that He takes away personal sins as well.

[6] Cf. May, *An Introduction to Moral Theology*, 186.

[7] CCC 404.

descendants."[8] It is a sin "contracted" but not "committed;" it is "a state and not an act," and in this sense it is only sin "in an analogical sense."[9]

As we saw in Chapter One, sin has left human nature in a weakened state subject to ignorance, suffering, bodily death, and the "inclination to evil that is called 'concupiscence.'"[10] Concupiscence is not sin itself, but the tendency to sin, especially with respect to self-assertion (pride), lust, and greed. It has been spoken of as "the tinder or fuel for sin" (*fomes peccati*), but it can be overcome by the grace of Christ.[11]

Personal sin, as opposed to original sin, involves a freely chosen "thought, word, deed, or omission"[12] that is contrary to the law of God. As a personal act, sin engages the intellect and the will,[13] and the person must freely choose to transgress the moral law. Sins are further distinguished as to whether they proceed from ignorance (due to lack of knowledge); weakness (giving in to strong passion or desire); or malice (emerging from an evil will or desire to harm).[14] As will soon become clear, most sexual sins proceed from weakness rather than malice, and in sins of passion, full and deliberate consent of the will may more easily be lacking.[15]

Sins engaged in freely and repetitively inevitably result in "perverse inclinations, which cloud conscience and corrupt the concrete judgment of good and evil."[16] These perverse inclinations to sin can also be called vices, which are habits that "have arisen through the repetition of acts."[17] Following St. John Cassian (c. 360–433)

---

[8] CCC 405.

[9] CCC 404.

[10] CCC 405.

[11] CCC 1264; cf. Council of Trent (1546): Denz-H, 1515.

[12] CCC 1853.

[13] Cf. Dominic Prümmer, O.P., *Handbook of Moral Theology*, trans. J.G. Nolan (New York: P.J. Kenedy & Sons, 1957), n. 158, p. 67.

[14] Ibid., no. 159, p. 68.

[15] Cf. Congregation for the Doctrine of the Faith [CDF], *Declaration on Certain Problems of Sexual Ethics*, *Persona humanae*, Dec. 29, 1975, no. 10, in *Vatican Council II: More Post Conciliar Documents*, ed. Austin Flannery, O.P. (Collegeville, MN: The Liturgical Press, 1982), 494.

[16] CCC 1865.

[17] Prümmer, no. 171, p. 75.

and St. Gregory the Great (c. 540–604), Church tradition has emphasized seven capital sins or vices; they are called "capital" because "they engender other sins, other vices."[18] These seven sins or vices are pride, avarice, envy, wrath, lust, gluttony, and sloth (or acedia).[19]

The inclusion of lust as one of the seven capital sins is significant. Lust is "the inordinate desire for sexual pleasure."[20] As a capital sin, it leads to other sins and a lessening of the love of God and neighbor. What other sins are engendered by lust? Frequently, it involves the exploitation of others for one's own gratification, which is a grave offense against charity and justice. Patterns of manipulation likewise come into play, and lustful people often employ deception to seduce others. Lust also can lead to reckless behavior, infidelity, unwanted pregnancies, and abortions. In cases of adultery, lust often gets entangled in other evils, such as betrayal, mendacity, anger, and violence. As can be seen, lust is a vice that engenders other moral offenses.

Students of literature know that the seven capital sins play a major role in the depictions of hell and purgatory in the *Divine Comedy* of Dante Alighieri (1265–1321). Lust follows limbo as the second circle of hell, and it is included with other sins of incontinence such as gluttony, avarice, wrath, and sloth. In purgatory, the lustful are placed in cornice 7 of the upper part, where, along with gluttons (cornice 6) and the covetous (cornice 5), they undergo purgation for excessive love of secondary goods.[21]

It is noteworthy that Dante understands sins of lust as less serious than sins of violence, fraud, and betrayal. This is because sins of the flesh involve a desire for actual goods, though in a disordered way. This might give the false impression that Dante does not consider sexual sins as all that serious. Such a conclusion, though, is untenable because Dante does place those guilty of sexual sins in hell, even

---

[18] CCC 1866.
[19] Cf. ibid.
[20] Prümmer, no. 174, p. 76.
[21] Cf. Dante, *The Divine Comedy 2: Purgatory*, trans. Dorothy Sayers (London: Penguin Books, 1955), 67.

if they are not in the lower circles of the *Inferno*. Moreover, the disorder caused by lust can lead to other more serious sins. For example, in Canto V of the *Inferno*, we find the adulterous lovers, Paolo and Francesca, who were murdered by Gianciotto (the deformed husband of Francesca and the brother of Paolo). The sin of lust of Paolo and Francesca is less serious than the fratricide of Gianciotto (who winds up in the first ring of the lowest circle of hell). Nevertheless, the adulterous lovers are still damned for their sin.

The Catholic Church distinguishes between less serious offenses, known as venial sins, and more serious sins, known as mortal sins. This distinction is found in 1 Jn 5:17: "All wrongdoing is sin, but there is sin which is not mortal." According to the Catholic Faith,[22] "mortal sin destroys charity in the heart of man by a grave violation of God's law; it turns man away from God, who is his ultimate end and his beatitude, by preferring an interior good to him." Venial sins allow the life of sanctifying grace or charity to continue, but they injure one's relationship with God and can make a person more prone to commit mortal sin.

Are sexual sins mortal sins? According to traditional Catholic manuals (theological textbooks), sexual sins do involve grave matter,[23] which, along with full knowledge and deliberate (or complete) consent, makes a sin mortal.[24] By "grave matter" we mean actions (or possibly omissions) that are serious enough to separate people from the state of grace and place them in danger of damnation.

Adultery is forbidden in the fifth commandment of the Decalogue (cf. Ex 20:14; Deut 5:18).[25] The gravity of adultery is

---

[22] CCC 1855.

[23] Prümmer, for example, defines lust as "the inordinate desire for sexual pleasure," and specifies it as "a mortal sin which admits no slight matter," no. 174, p. 76. See also, Fr. Heribert Jone, *Moral Theology*, trans. and adapted Fr. Urban Adelman, O.F.M. Cap. [1961] (Rockford, IL: Tan Books and Publishers, 1993): "All directly voluntary sexual pleasure is mortally sinful outside of marriage," no. 223, p. 146. Worth noting also is the response of the Holy Office given in 1661 regarding sexual solicitation by a priest confessor which states that "there is no lightness of matter in sexual matters" (*in rebus venereis non detur parvitas materiae*): Denz.-H. 2013.

[24] Cf. CCC 1857–1859.

[25] Jews and most Protestants consider the prohibition of adultery as the seventh commandment because of a different numbering scheme.

witnessed to by Lev 20:10, which enjoins the death penalty for men and women who commit this sin. The Old Testament likewise issues strong condemnations of Onanism (Gen 38:9); incest (Lev 20:11–12, 19–21); homosexual acts (Gen 19:1–13; Lev 18:22, 20:13); bestiality (Ex 22:18; Deut 27:21; Lev 20:15–16); and pre-marital sex (Deut 22:13–21, 28–29). In the New Testament, adultery, fornication, and sodomy are listed as sins that prevent inheritance in the kingdom of God (cf. 1 Cor 6:9–10). Sensuality (*aselgeia*) and impurity (*akatharsia*) are likewise condemned (cf. Gal 5:20 and Eph 5:3), and Jesus warns about lusting in one's heart (Mt 5:28).

In spite of these strong biblical condemnations of various sexual sins, some Catholic theologians have tried to minimize the gravity of certain sins of the flesh.[26] Others have tried to argue that mortal sin is only involved if the sexual sins contribute to a negative fundamental option against God.[27] Still others minimize the seriousness of sexual sins because they have become so common and culturally acceptable today. If "everybody's doing it," how can it be so wrong?

In the chapters that follow, different types of sexual sins will be discussed, such as pornography, masturbation, homosexual acts, fornication, cohabitation, and contraception. These sins are so widespread in our present culture that many people find it difficult to understand how they are sinful at all. Still others recognize these acts as sinful, but they sometimes indulge in them out of weakness or passion. For some people, striving to overcome sins of the flesh is a long and difficult struggle. Many fall into patterns of addictive behavior and suffer from feelings of failure, shame, and self-

---

[26] Fr. Charles Curran, for example, has stated that sins of masturbation usually do not involve grave matter, and he also has argued that homosexual acts in some contexts "can in a certain sense be objectively morally acceptable;" cf. "Some Background on Father Curran's Case," *Origins*, Vol. 15; No. 41 (Nov. 27, 1986), 669.

[27] The fundamental option theory tends to understand mortal sin only in terms of a basic orientation against God and neighbor, and it frequently denies that individual acts can be mortal sins. The fundamental option theory has been criticized by the Congregation for the Doctrine of the Faith in *Persona Humana* (1975), no. 10 and by John Paul II in *Veritatis Splendor* (1993), nn. 65–70.

reproach. Even prayerful and good people can develop patterns of sexual addiction. Such people often believe they are alone in their hidden passions and attractions.

Here it must be emphasized that any discussion of sin must be complemented by the message of God's forgiveness. Jesus came to call sinners, and the Catholic Church is well aware of the weaknesses of human nature. Those who "miss the mark" in sexual matters must humbly and sincerely ask God for mercy, forgiveness, and the grace to resist temptations in the future. The Church also knows that "total free consent may easily be lacking in sins of sex" and "prudence and caution are therefore needed in passing any judgment on a person's responsibility."[28]

Catholics who struggle with sexual sins and humbly turn to the sacrament of Confession for forgiveness are in a far better spiritual state than those who, either out of habit or moral insensitivity, deny the sinfulness of pornography, masturbation, fornication, and other such actions. The worst thing a Catholic priest can do to a person confessing sexual sins is to tell the penitent that such actions are not sinful.[29] As Fr. Benedict Groeschel has observed: "It is not the job of a doctor or clergyman to tell someone that what is wrong is right."[30] God is ready to forgive those who are sorry for their sins, but He does not forgive those who refuse to acknowledge their sins and who persist in immoral behavior.

---

[28] Congregation for the Doctrine of the Faith, *Declaration on Certain Questions concerning Sexual Ethics, Persona Humana* (1975), n. 10 in Austin Flannery, O.P., ed., *Vatican II: More Post Conciliar Documents* (Collegeville, MN: The Liturgical Press, 1982), 494.

[29] Benedict J. Groeschel, O.F.M. Cap., *The Courage to Be Chaste* (New York: Paulist Press, 1985), 49.

[30] Ibid.

CHAPTER FIVE

PORNOGRAPHY

The eyes are one the greatest gifts of God. To be able to see the world with its lights and shadows, its colors and shapes; to behold the faces of those we love and gaze upon the beauty of creation — these are all blessings that should inspire thanks and praise from our hearts. The language of Scripture is full of images that relate to our eyes: light and darkness; vision and blindness; and the heavenly Jerusalem ablaze with radiance, gleaming like jasper, "having the glory of God" (cf. Rev 21: 11).

Yet Scripture also warns about "the lust of the flesh and the lust of the eyes" (1 Jn 2:16). Our Lord condemns not only the act of adultery, but also the "adultery of the heart," which occurs when a woman is looked upon with lust (cf. Mt 5:28). Indeed, it would be better to tear out our eye and throw it away than to sin and have our whole body "go into hell" (Mt 5:30). Christ likewise emphasizes the importance of the eye to the soul in these words:

> The eye is the lamp of the body. So, if your eye is sound, your whole body will be full of light; but if your eye is not sound, your whole body will be full of darkness. If then the light in you is darkness, how great is the darkness! (Mt 6:22–23)

As we saw in Chapter Two on the "theology of the body," Adam and Eve were naked without shame until their fall from God's grace. After their sin, "the eyes of both were opened, and they knew that they were naked; and they sewed fig leaves together and made themselves aprons" (Gen 3:7). Prior to the fall, as John Paul II notes, Adam and Eve possessed "interior innocence as purity of heart," which "made it impossible somehow for one to be reduced by the other to the level of a mere object."[1] Nakedness was experienced without shame because "they were mutually conscious of the nuptial meaning of their bodies, in which the freedom of the gift is expressed and all the interior riches of the person as subject are manifested."[2]

The fall changes all this, but it does not entirely remove the spousal meaning of the body from the human heart. As John Paul II explains:

> After original sin, man and woman will lose the grace of original innocence. The discovery of the nuptial meaning of the body will cease to be for them a simple reality of revelation and grace. However, this meaning will remain as a commitment given to man by the ethos of the gift, inscribed in the depths of the human heart, as a distant echo of original innocence. From the nuptial meaning human love in its interior truth and subjective authenticity will be formed. Through the veil of shame, man will continually rediscover himself as the guardian of the mystery of the subject, that is, of the freedom of the gift. This is so as to defend it from any reduction to the position of mere object.[3]

Because of the effects of original sin, God's grace is needed to elevate and purify the way we look upon our bodies as male and female. When Christ establishes the holiness and indissolubility of marriage as the norm for His followers (cf. Mt 19:4–6), He uses the way man and woman were constituted by the Creator "from the beginning" as the point of reference. As one theologian writes:

> Clearly for His followers, in His Church, Jesus was restoring the primordial order of Paradise, where love, not violence,

---

[1] John Paul II, General audience of Feb. 20, 1980; TOB, 75.
[2] Ibid.
[3] Ibid.

rules and marriage becomes the sign of God's love that it was originally intended to be.[4]

The covenant of marriage, therefore, reestablishes something of the state of Eden prior to the fall. The husband and wife can be "naked without shame" in the presence of each other because the grace of the sacrament has restored the nuptial meaning of their bodies.

As explained in Chapter Three, one legitimate purpose of marriage is to serve as the "remedy of concupiscence" (*remedium concupiscentiae*), that is, as a means for channeling strong sexual desires away from sinful actions like masturbation and fornication.[5] Though "the remedy of concupiscence" might be a "secondary end" of marriage, it nevertheless relates to the subject of pornography. The lust of the eyes that emerges from concupiscence must be overcome in service of marital love. For those who are married this means that they cannot look upon other naked bodies with lust because their sexual urges are directed to the unitive and procreative ends of their own marriage. Those who are not married should recognize that only married couples have the privilege of looking upon each other's naked bodies in a manner that is likely to arouse sexual passion. And even in marriage, the husband and the wife are not to look upon each other's bodies with sinful lust. This would reduce the spouse to an object for sexual gratification, which, as we saw in Chapter Three, demeans the true beauty and purpose of conjugal love.

Art versus Pornography

Those who are lovers of art are sensitive to the beauty of the human body. In the ancient Greco-Roman world, there was a certain glorification of the human physique in sculpture that reemerged at the time of the European Renaissance. The Catholic Church has been

---

[4] John M. McDermott, S.J., "Science, Sexual Morality, and Church Teaching: Another Look at *Humanae Vitae*," *Irish Theological Quarterly* 70 (2005), 250.

[5] Cf. 1 Cor 7:9 and canon 1013 of the 1917 *Codex Iuris Canonici* (Westminster, MD: The Newman Press, 1964), 341.

a patron of the arts for centuries. What guidelines should be given with regard to art and nudity?

John Paul II, in his general audiences of April 15, 22, and 29 and May 6, 1981,[6] and in his April 8, 1994 homily for the unveiling of the restored Michelangelo frescoes in the Sistine Chapel, articulated a few basic points that can serve as a guide for distinguishing art from pornography. These can be summarized as follows:

1. The aesthetic prototype of the human body in art cannot be detached from the meaning of the human person.

2. We must avoid "looking lustfully" at artistic representations or photographs of the human body.

3. We must avoid looking upon anonymous subjects of photographic art as objects for enjoyment rather than as persons.

4. We must respect the human body as gift in reference to its masculinity and femininity.

5. While the human body, in its nakedness, can be a subject of art, there must be moral and not simply aesthetic sensitivity.

6. There is a proper sense of shame or modesty with respect to the human body: "Man does not wish to become an object for others through his own anonymous nakedness. Nor does he wish the other to become an object for him in a similar way."

7. "Pornovision" and "pornography" take place "when the limit of shame is overstepped, that is, of personal sensitivity with regard to what is connected with the human body with its nakedness."

8. The Church's resistance to pornovision and pornography "is not the effect of a puritanical mentality or ... narrow

---

[6] Cf. TOB, 222–228.

moralism" or "Manichaeism." Rather, it is a response to the dignity of the human person and "the eloquence of the human body."

9. In true art with the human body as the subject, there is an element of sublimation which "leads the viewer, through the body, to the whole mystery of man ... we do not feel drawn by their content to 'look lustfully,' which the Sermon on the Mount speaks about."

10. As Pope Paul VI teaches in *Humanae Vitae*, we must "create an atmosphere favorable to education in chastity."

11. The body is the *kenosis*, or self-emptying, of God; God is the source of the integral beauty of the human body. Respect for this principle was articulated at Nicea II (787).

12. The Sistine Chapel is "the sanctuary of the theology of the human body."[7]

The Magisterium on Pornography

Why is pornography wrong? In Sirach 9:8, we are told: "Turn away your eyes from a shapely woman, and do not look intently at beauty belonging to another." In 1 Jn 2:6, we are warned about the lust of the eyes and the lust of the flesh. In Gal 5:19–20, St. Paul lists impurity (*akatharsia*) and licentiousness or lustfulness (*aselgeia*) among "the works of the flesh." Those who are clean of heart (cf. Mt 5:8) are blessed, while those who look with lust upon women are condemned.

Looking upon the human body with lust has become all the more accessible through modern means of media and social communication. In 1968, Pope Paul VI recognized the need to condemn publicly everything "which arouses men's baser passions and encourages low moral standards, as well as every obscenity in the written word and every form of indecency on stage and on screen."[8] Pope

---

[7] John Paul II, Homily of April 8, 1994. http://www.vatican.va/holy_father/ john_paul_ii/homilies/1994/documents/hf_jpii_hom_19940408_restauri-sistina_en. html.

[8] Paul VI, *Humanae Vitae* (1968), n. 22.

John Paul II saw pornography as an offense against the dignity of women because it considers the human being "not as a person but as a thing, as an object of trade, at the service of selfish interest and mere pleasure."[9]

In a similar vein, the *Catechism of the Catholic Church* speaks of pornography as an offense against chastity "because it perverts the sexual act."[10] Moreover, it "does grave injury to the dignity of its participants (actors, vendors, the public), since each one becomes an object of base pleasure and illicit profit for others."[11] Pornography likewise "immerses all who are involved in the illusion of a fantasy world" and is "a grave offense."[12] Families, therefore, have a right to be protected from pornography.[13]

The connection between pornography and other sexual sins, such as masturbation, should be obvious, because pornography often leads to autoerotic stimulation. Pornography is the enemy of modesty and purity of heart.[14] It degrades human dignity and preys upon vulnerable victims, especially women.

Many people, however, fail to see the harms of pornography. But there is ample evidence of the link of pornography to sexual addiction and psychosexual dysfunction.[15] There is likewise evidence of the connection between pornography and violent crime, rape, the exploitation of women, sado-masochism, sexual deviation, domestic assaults, and reduction of human compassion.[16] Equally frightening is the persistent presence of pornography as a factor in the sexual abuse of minors.[17]

---

[9] John Paul II, *Familiaris Consortio* (1981), n. 24.

[10] CCC 2354.

[11] Ibid.

[12] Ibid.; cf. CCC 2396.

[13] Cf. CCC 2211.

[14] Cf. CCC 2520.

[15] Cf. Richard Wetzel, M.D., *Sexual Wisdom: A Guide for Parents, Young Adults, Educators and Physicians* (Ann Arbor, MI: Proctor Publications, 1998), 176–178.

[16] Cf. Dr. Victor Cline, "A Psychologist's View of Pornography," in *The Case against Pornography,* edited by Donald E. Wildmon (Wheaton, IL: Victor Books, 1986), 43–56.

[17] Cf. Wildmon, 57–77.

Beyond the social and psychological harms of pornography are the spiritual effects. As Bishop Loverde of the Diocese of Arlington, Virginia, has noted, pornography damages man's "template" for the supernatural.[18] Those who indulge in pornography distort their perception of reality and cripple their ability to sense the presence and action of God.

Overcoming Addiction to Pornography

Those who are addicted to pornography often have a long and painful process of breaking free of this vice. They should begin their recovery by: (1) Recognizing pornography as objectively sinful for all the reasons outlined earlier; (2) avoiding the near occasions of sin; (3) if the addiction involves the use of the Internet, purging their computer of all pornography links; (4) making ample use of prayer and fasting; (5) in some cases, seeking pastoral or even psychological counseling for help in overcoming their addiction; (6) making frequent use of the sacrament of confession; (7) cultivating wholesome forms of entertainment and recreation that are not in any way linked to pornography or sexual stimulation; and (8) developing healthy friendships removed from sexual exploitation or indulgence.

Bishop Robert W. Finn of the Diocese of Kansas City-St. Joseph, Missouri, has also provided some excellent practical advice for responding to the problem of pornography in a pastoral letter entitled, *Blessed Are the Pure of Heart* (Feb. 21, 2007).[19] For those struggling with pornography, he suggests, among others, the following steps: (1) Face and name the problem; (2) avoid a secretive or enticing environment; (3) eliminate pornographic materials; (4) be good stewards of our time; (5) know our weaknesses; (6) commit to daily prayer; (7) be strengthened by the

---

[18] Bishop Paul S. Loverde, *Bought with a Price: Pornography and the Attack on the Living Temple of God* (2006). This pastoral letter can be found on the Web site of the Diocese of Arlington (www.arlingtondiocese.org/offices/communications/boughtprice.html).

[19] The pastoral letter is available online at http:///www.diocese-kcsj.org/Bishop-Finn/ pastoral-07.htm.

Holy Sacrifice of the Mass; (8) make a daily examination of conscience and go to confession frequently; (9) make use of good spiritual reading and cultivate the awareness of God's presence; (10) develop a plan to grow in the virtues of temperance, modesty, purity, and chastity; (11) seek support from friends or a spiritual director; and (12) seek support from the Blessed Mother and saints like St. Joseph and St. Maria Goretti.[20]

To these, we might add some other basic steps, such as using computers in public places and obtaining filters that eliminate pornographic items. Also, men need to cultivate a protective rather than exploitive attitude toward women. In some cases, men need to consider how they would react if other men were looking at their sisters or daughters the way they are looking at women displayed in pornographic magazines and videos.

---

[20] The presentation by way of numbers is mine and not that of Bishop Finn, but I am relying on the points made in his pastoral letter.

CHAPTER SIX

MASTURBATION

When I was in graduate school in the mid-1970s, the subject of masturbation once came up in a conversation I had with a professor. According to this professor (and priest!), masturbation was not a sin at all. Rather, the sin was to teach that masturbation *was* a sin because such a teaching was tantamount to "terrorizing children."

Needless to say, I was a bit shocked by this position, but I daresay this particular professor was not alone in his estimation. Several years ago, a priest informed me that he hardly heard masturbation being confessed anymore in the sacrament of reconciliation. He asked me whether I thought people were masturbating less or whether people no longer considered it a sin. I told him I suspected it was the latter.

Today, many people believe masturbation is simply a normal activity of adolescent self-discovery, and they likewise believe it is acceptable for adults to masturbate if they are single and lack a sexual partner. The normalcy of masturbation is often reinforced in health and sex education classes in public (and sometimes Catholic!) schools. Why, then, does the Catholic Church maintain that masturbation is a sin?

Something should first be said about the word "normal." What is normal might refer to something that is statistically common or typical. In this sense, many social scientists feel confident in describing masturbation as "normal," especially for adolescent boys. Statistically, they might be correct, but it should be noted that what is "normal" in the statistical sense is not always good. It is "normal" in the statistical sense for people to get sick, lose their tempers, or to lie, but none of these conditions or behaviors should be described as good. People frequently get speeding or parking tickets, they arrive late for work or school, and they often engage in gossip. None of these actions is good.

It is much the same with masturbation. In light of our fallen nature and the inclination to sin known as concupiscence, it is easy to understand how sexual self-stimulation can be a persistent temptation, especially for those who feel depressed, unloved, or closed in upon themselves. Moreover, modern culture is full of sexual images that often emerge unexpectedly. Even when walking down a city street or strolling through a shopping mall, sexually stimulating images can present themselves to the imagination through advertisements, modes of dress, and suggestive music. All these stimulations are received by the mind through the senses and can reemerge as temptations later in the day or at night. We should also be mindful of the reality of the Evil One, who can use these natural stimulations as an opening to tempt us into sin.

Masturbation, therefore, can be understood as "normal" only in the sense that sin is "normal" for human beings weakened by the material effects of original sin. Both "the moral sense of the faithful" and the Magisterium of the Church agree that "masturbation is an intrinsically and gravely disordered action."[1] Why then is this sin so common in the world today? In addition to the "weakness implanted in man by original sin," there are other factors such as "the loss of the sense of God," the "commercialization of vice," and the "neglect of modesty."[2]

Modern psychology can help us understand factors that can diminish the responsibility of those who masturbate, but "the

---

[1] CDF, *Persona Humana*, 9.

[2] CDF, *Persona Humana*, 9. Earlier magisterial condemnations of masturbation include the 1054 letter of Pope Leo IX to Peter Damian (Denz.-H, 687-688) and the 1929 decree of the Holy Office rejecting the moral liceity of direct masturbation for obtaining a medical specimen (Denz-H, 3684). Masturbation also was likely included under the procuring of a "pollution" mentioned in the 1665 censuring by the Holy Office of various laxist theses (Denz-H, 2044).

absence of grave responsibility must not always be presumed."[3] Instead, pastors and confessors must judge culpability on a case-by-case basis taking into account factors such as "affective immaturity, force of acquired habit, conditions of anxiety, or other psychological or social factors that can lessen, if not reduce to a minimum, moral culpability."[4]

One particularly delicate question is whether those who struggle with the sin of masturbation should refrain from receiving Holy Communion. Of course, those who are conscious of grave sin are not to receive the Eucharist without prior sacramental confession "unless a grave reason is present and there is no opportunity of confessing."[5] With respect to the sin of masturbation, the act itself is gravely wrong. The question is whether the other two conditions for a mortal sin are present: namely, full knowledge and complete consent.[6] Those who are well catechized in the faith should have full knowledge that masturbation is grievously wrong. The consent to masturbate, however, must be "sufficiently deliberate to be a personal choice."[7]

The force of habit can diminish the completeness of one's consent to the act. This is especially true at night or early in the morning when a person might be half asleep. Before receiving Holy Communion, an examination of conscience should be made to discern whether full and deliberate consent of the will was given to the prior act or acts of masturbation. A good confessor or spiritual director is sometimes needed to help in this discernment, especially if masturbation proves to be a persistent habit. The worst thing, though, a confessor can tell a person is that masturbation is not a sin. Such counsel is not only wrong objectively, but it will likely help to fixate a person even more deeply in the masturbatory habit.

---

[3] CDF, *Persona Humana*, 9.
[4] CCC 2352.
[5] CIC, canon 916.
[6] Cf. CCC 1859.
[7] CCC 1859.

Some people agree that masturbation is wrong, but they have trouble understanding it as a gravely disordered act. One reason for this is the loss of respect for the sanctity of the sexual gift. If sexual relations are primarily for pleasure, then it seems reasonable for this pleasure to be sought in a solitary as well as mutual fashion. The use, however, of the sexual faculty outside of marriage "is essentially contrary to its purpose."[8] Acts of masturbation are neither unitive nor procreative. They reduce the sexual gift to a source of solitary pleasure, and they embody the vices of uncleanness and unchastity that are condemned in the New Testament (cf. Gal. 5:20 and Eph. 5:3).

It might be true that some people who masturbate do so because they are lonely and would much rather unite with a spouse than engage in erotic self-stimulation. Such loneliness might help to explain why masturbation takes place, but it does not justify it. Those who are lonely need to develop friendships with others and intimacy with God. Moreover, masturbation is often linked to other sexual sins such as pornography and impure thoughts. Masturbation likewise can move individuals toward the use of prostitutes or the sexual exploitation of others. Although it can be a symptom of psychological immaturity, it can also be indicative of a general pattern of sexual self-indulgence that, like pornography, dulls one's sensitivity to God and the needs of others.

Those who find themselves struggling with masturbation need to develop a spiritual plan to achieve self-control with God's grace. Habitual masturbation is "a problem for which a counselor, spiritual director, or a confessor can be of considerable help."[9] Such people can help a person "understand the causes of this behavior, which are often habitual or in response to emotional stress or unexamined underlying attitudes."[10] In many cases, adolescent habits of masturbation are overcome with maturity. Over time, chaste

---

[8] *Persona Humana*, 9.

[9] U.S. Conference of Catholic Bishops, *United States Catholic Catechism for Adults* (Washington, DC: U.S Conference of Catholic Bishops, 2006), 406.

[10] Ibid.

friendships with those of the opposite sex replace self-absorbed fantasies. In some cases, however, habits of masturbation can persist into adulthood, even among married men and women.

Why do habits of masturbation persist? Fr. John Harvey, O.S.F.S., notes that "there is a close correlation between moods of depression, anger, loneliness, and sexual fantasy, and the temptation to masturbate."[11] In times such as these, "one should make a special effort of mind and heart to bring oneself back into the real world, and particularly to concentrate on the needs of others."[12] In extreme cases, something analogous to the Twelve Steps of Alcoholics Anonymous should be used. When masturbation is eliminated, there is a void that needs to be filled by the "experience of *real* relationships with God in prayer, and with other persons."[13]

Ultimately, masturbation must be understood not only as a sin but also as a sign of emotional emptiness and desperation. The love of God is needed to fill the hearts of those who seek release through erotic self-stimulation. This love is God's grace, which heals and elevates the human person from wretchedness and brokenness to wholeness and peace.

---

[11] John F. Harvey, "The Pastoral Problem of Masturbation," *Linacre Quarterly*, vol. 60, no. 2 (May 1993), 43.

[12] Ibid.

[13] Ibid., 45.

CHAPTER SEVEN

HOMOSEXUALITY

It seems impossible to discuss the issue of homosexuality without encountering strong reactions. A former colleague once told me that I was "homophobic" because I agreed with the *Catechism* that homosexual acts are immoral.[1] I came to the conclusion that he used the word "homophobic" to describe anyone who does not believe homosexual acts are the moral equivalent of heterosexual acts and who does not place homosexual unions on equal footing with heterosexual marriage.[2]

Many people today have difficulty with the Catholic Church's teaching that homosexual acts cannot be moral under any circumstances.[3] "Human beings need love," a student once told me, "and why should homosexuals be denied the same freedom to love as heterosexuals?" The issue is often framed as a question of non-discrimination against minorities. Homosexuals are depicted as a persecuted minority, and very few people wish to be called persecutors of minorities.

By way of response, it should be noted that there is a big difference between persecuting people because of their race or ethnic group and judging certain actions or lifestyles to be immoral. There is nothing immoral about being a certain skin color or ethnicity. To discriminate against people because of their race or ethnic background *is* unjust. Active homosexuality, however, involves

---

[1] Cf. CCC 2357.

[2] Of course, there might be genuine cases of "homophobia" manifested by hateful attitudes, words, and actions directed against those struggling with homosexual attractions.

[3] Cf. ibid.

behavior, not skin color or some other factor that is morally neutral. The Catholic Church teaches that "every sign of unjust discrimination" against homosexuals "should be avoided."[4] It is not unjust discrimination to affirm what Scripture, Tradition, and the natural law teach about the immoral character of homoerotic actions. No one can claim a right to engage in immoral behavior. The question then is *why* does the Catholic Church teach that homosexual acts are wrong?

The Origins of Homosexuality

In order to understand the Catholic Church's moral doctrine on this subject, the question of the origin of homosexuality must be addressed. Many people believe that homosexuals are "born that way," and, therefore, homosexual relations are perfectly normal for those who have inherited the homosexual or "gay" gene. Personal testimonies of homosexuals often lend support to this thesis. Many homosexuals say they knew they were gay from their early childhood, or at least they knew they were "different."

What does science say about all this? According to the Catholic Medical Association (CMA), a number of authors have reviewed the studies that allegedly support "a biological basis for same-sex attraction." These authors have found that these studies "not only do not prove a genetic basis for same-sex attraction, they do not even claim to have scientific evidence for such a claim."[5] If homosexuality were genetically determined, then we should expect identical twins to always both be either homosexual or heterosexual. Yet a 1991 study revealed that 52 percent (29 out of 56) of identical twins surveyed were both homosexual. This study, though, was flawed because the subjects were recruited from advertisements in homosexual journals.[6] A subsequent study by the same researchers

---

[4] CCC 2358.

[5] Catholic Medical Association, *Homosexuality and Hope* (A.D. 2000), I, 1. This statement can be found on the Web site of the Catholic Medical Association, viz., www.cathmed.org/publications/homosexuality.htm.

[6] Nicanor Pier Giorgio Austriaco, O.P., "The Myth of the Gay Gene," *Homiletic and Pastoral Review*, vol. CIV, no. 3 (December 2003), 30.

in 2000 revealed that only 20 percent of identical twins are both homosexual when one or the other has same-sex attraction.[7] If homosexuality were genetically determined, we would expect both twins to be homosexual 100 percent of the time.

The scientific facts seem to argue in favor of environmental causes for homosexuality rather than genetic. But even if there were a genetic predisposition toward homosexuality, this would not mean that homosexual acts are therefore good. Some people might have a genetic predisposition toward alcoholism or violence. This does not mean that heavy drinking and violent behavior are good.

If the causes of homosexuality are environmental, is it possible to reverse the condition? The Catholic Medical Association points to "a failure to identify positively with one's own sex" as a major factor in developing homosexual tendencies.[8] For males with homosexual tendencies, alienation from the father in early childhood is often a common cause, especially when combined with an overprotective, needy, or demanding mother.[9] For females with homosexual tendencies, there is frequently an emotionally unavailable mother[10] or fear and mistrust of men because of bad experiences.[11] For both male and female persons with homosexual inclinations, factors such as sadness, loneliness, and sexual trauma in childhood can all play a role.[12] For males, a lack of hand/eye coordination, failure in sports, and subsequent teasing often contribute to a weak masculine identity and homosexual tendencies.[13]

---

[7] Ibid.

[8] *Homosexuality and Hope*, I, 3.

[9] Ibid., I, 2.

[10] Ibid.

[11] Cf. Richard Fitzgibbons, M.D., "The Origins and Healing of Homosexual Attraction and Behaviors," in Appendix I to Fr. John F. Harvey, O.S.S.F., *The Truth about Homosexuality: The Cry of the Faithful* (San Francisco: Ignatius Press, 1996), 315–316; see also pp. 259–301 for various case studies of women who developed same-sex attractions.

[12] Cf. Fitzgibbons, Appendix I, 309–322.

[13] Cf. *Homosexuality and Hope*, I, 2, and Fitzgibbons, Appendix I, 312–313.

When these and other causes for same-sex attraction are recognized, it is possible to pursue "reparative therapy," which can result in either total or partial freedom from homosexual traits.[14] Robert Spitzer, M.D., from Columbia University, who was instrumental in removing homosexuality from the American Psychiatric Association's list of mental disorders, now admits that there is evidence of many people moving from homosexuality toward heterosexuality through therapy.[15] Reparative therapy is not always successful, but, for many, it provides genuine healing of deep emotional wounds and opens the way to a fuller, happier, and more peaceful life. When persons with homosexual tendencies, however, are told that they were "born that way," and encouraged to engage in homoerotic acts, there is little hope for healing and moral growth.

Catholic moralists debate whether there is always a moral responsibility to seek reparative therapy in cases of homosexuality. What cannot be debated, however, is the need to live in accord with the moral law. Those who have deep-seated homosexual tendencies "are called to chastity."[16] They are also "called to fulfill God's will in their lives and, if they are Christians, to unite to the sacrifice of the Lord's Cross the difficulties they may encounter from their condition."[17] Those struggling with homosexual temptations must strive for "self-mastery." As the *Catechism* teaches, "by the support of disinterested friendship, by prayer and sacramental grace, they can and should gradually and resolutely approach Christian perfection."[18]

Sacred Scripture, Natural Law, and Homosexuality

The Catholic Church believes that Sacred Scripture "presents homosexual acts as acts of grave depravity."[19] Gen 19:1–29 (the story

---

[14] Ibid. I, 5.
[15] Ibid.
[16] CCC 2359.
[17] Ibid., 2358.
[18] Ibid., 2359.
[19] Ibid., 2357.

of Sodom and Gomorrah), Rom 1:24–27, 1 Cor 6:10, and 1 Tim
1:10 may all be cited to support this.[20] Although some have tried
to deny the Scriptural repudiation of homosexual acts, an objective
reading of the Bible will show that "nowhere is there any approval
of homosexual unions."[21] In Lev 18:22, we are told that it is "an
abomination" for a man to lie "with a male as with a woman" (cf.
Lev 20:13); St. Paul, in 1 Cor 6:9–10, lists homosexual acts among
the sins that deprive people of the kingdom of God; Rom 1:26–27
points to homosexual behavior as a manifestation of spiritual blindness; and 1 Tim 1:10 includes homosexual sinners among the "unholy and profane" who are opposed to "sound doctrine." Read
within the light of the Church's living Tradition, these passages reveal a "clear consistency" on "the moral issue of homosexual behavior."[22] Thus, what the Catholic Church teaches about the
immorality of homosexual acts is based "on the solid foundation
of a constant Biblical testimony."[23]

The Church also believes that homosexual acts are "intrinsically disordered" and "contrary to the natural law."[24] The natural
law is the law of "right reason."[25] It expresses "the original moral
sense which enables man to discern by reason the good and the evil,
the truth and the lie."[26] The natural law likewise reflects the "order
of creation" and teaches human beings how to pursue goodness
and attain their end.[27] From the perspective of the natural law, homosexual acts "close the sexual act to the gift of life," and "they do
not proceed from a genuine affective and sexual complementarity.[28]

---

[20] Cf. CCC, footnote 141, in reference to CCC 2357.

[21] Fr. John F. Harvey, O.S.F.S., "Contemporary Theology Views," in John R. Cavanaugh, M.D., *Counseling the Homosexual* (Huntington, IN: Our Sunday Visitor,
1977), 227.

[22] Congregation for the Doctrine of the Faith, *Letter to the Bishops of the Catholic
Church on the Pastoral Care of Homosexual Persons*, n. 5.

[23] Ibid.

[24] CCC 2357.

[25] Cf. CCC 1956.

[26] CCC 1954.

[27] Cf. CCC 1955.

[28] CCC 2357.

The order of creation manifests a complementarity between the male and female bodies, and sexual intercourse between a man and a woman can produce new life. Homosexual acts are "intrinsically disordered" and sterile. They are contrary to the natural order of creation manifested in the sexual complementarity of men and women. It is not surprising that there are numerous physical and medical harms linked to active homosexuality.[29] This is why St. Paul states that men who have committed "shameless acts with men" have received "in their own persons the due penalty for their error" (Rom 1:27).

The Moral Evaluation of Homosexual Acts

When the Church teaches that the homosexual inclination is "objectively disordered,"[30] she is not saying that homosexual people lack human dignity. People are not guilty of sin simply because they have homosexual desires. The homosexual inclination, however, "is a more or less strong tendency ordered toward an intrinsic moral evil; and thus the inclination itself must be seen as an objective disorder."[31] Because the homosexual orientation is directed toward acts that are intrinsically immoral, it can never be understood as a positive good in itself. God, however, can bring good out of human weaknesses and temptations when they are overcome by the power of his grace. This is why homosexuals are counseled to unite "the difficulties they may encounter from their condition" to the "sacrifice of the Lord's Cross."[32]

People who suffer from homosexual tendencies often have difficulty perceiving their desires as disordered. Moreover, they are often reassured that homosexual acts are morally acceptable and that those who disapprove of these acts are the ones with a prob-

---

[29] Cf. Christopher Wolfe, "Homosexuality in American Public Life," in Christopher Wolfe, ed. *Same-Sex Matters: The Challenge of Homosexuality* (Dallas, TX: Spence Publishing Company, 2000), 12; see also, Dr. Paul Cameron, *The Gay Nineties: What the Empirical Evidence Reveals about Homosexuality* (Franklin, TN: Adroit Press, 1993), 38–59.

[30] CCC 2538.

[31] Congregation for the Doctrine of the Faith, *On the Pastoral Care of Homosexuals*, 3.

[32] CCC 2538.

lem. Thus, they frequently become even more fixated in homosexual patterns of behavior. Because of original sin and concupiscence, human beings have a tendency to rationalize immoral behavior, especially when there is pleasure or emotional satisfaction involved. The desire for love and affirmation is deeply rooted in human nature. Homosexual relations can appear to express genuine affection, and, as a consequence, we are reluctant to criticize them because we recognize the basic human need for love.

The moral evaluation of homosexual acts, however, cannot be based on subjective feelings. The desire for love and affection cannot be satisfied in harmful and immoral ways. From the objective viewpoint of Scripture and the natural law, the Catholic Church believes that homosexual activity, like every moral disorder, "prevents one's own fulfillment and happiness by acting contrary to the creative wisdom of God."[33] Those with strong homosexual tendencies often have deep wounds of insecurity, as well as collateral symptoms such as narcissism, anger, and aggression. Homoerotic inclinations can emerge from profound psychological problems,[34] and those who justify homosexual activity frequently prevent people from seeking the help they need. The justification of homosexual acts is a form of false compassion because human beings can never benefit from immoral behavior. Homosexual relations, like pornography and masturbation, can provide a deceptive sense of enjoyment and release; but because they violate the moral law, they can never be conducive to moral and spiritual development.

The Catholic Church teaches that the culpability of those who engage in homosexual acts "will be judged prudently."[35] The need for prudence in this regard is based on the recognition of the complex psychological factors involved. It is never permitted, however, "to employ any pastoral method or theory to provide justification" for homosexual actions.[36] Such acts "are intrinsically

---

[33] Ibid., 7.
[34] *Homosexuality and Hope*, 2.
[35] Congregation for the Doctrine of the Faith, *Persona Humana*, 8.
[36] Ibid.

disordered and may never be approved in any way whatsoever."[37] Any pastoral program that seeks to help those with homosexual tendencies must be clear about authentic Catholic teaching. As the Congregation for the Doctrine of the Faith taught in 1986:

> No authentic pastoral program will include organizations in which homosexual persons associate with each other without clearly stating that homosexual activity is immoral. A truly pastoral approach will appreciate the need for homosexual persons to avoid the near occasions of sin. We heartily encourage programs where these dangers are avoided. But we wish to make it clear that departure from the Church's teaching or silence about it is neither caring nor pastoral. Only what is true can ultimately be pastoral. The neglect of the Church's position prevents homosexual men and women from receiving the care they need and deserve.[38]

The teaching of the Catholic Church on homosexuality resonates with the views of many other Christians, as well as traditional Jews, Muslims, and members of other religions. Unfortunately, many countries are promoting laws that grant civil recognition to homosexual unions. In light of this, the Congregation for the Doctrine of the Faith (CDF), in 2003, issued a document entitled, *Considerations regarding Proposals to Give Legal Recognition to Unions between Homosexual Persons.* The CDF makes it clear that "there are absolutely no grounds for considering homosexual unions to be in any way similar or even remotely analogous to God's plan for marriage and family."[39] The document also speaks of the dangers involved in allowing children to be adopted by homosexual couples.[40] Furthermore, Catholic legislators are reminded of their "moral duty" to voice opposition to any legislative initiatives aimed

---

[37] Ibid.
[38] *On the Pastoral Care of Homosexual Persons*, 15.
[39] Congregation for the Doctrine of the Faith, *Considerations regarding to Proposals to Give Legal Recognition to Unions between Homosexual Persons* (2003), 4.
[40] Ibid., 7.

at granting "legal recognition of homosexual unions."[41] When legal recognition of such unions is already in force, a Catholic politician must voice opposition and seek ways to lessen the harm done by such a law.[42]

Homosexuality and the Priesthood

In recent years, the Catholic Church in the U.S.A. has endured what is sometimes called "the clergy sex abuse crisis." Although individual cases of minors abused by Catholic clergy were known in the past, it was the year 2002 that brought the situation to the public eye. Many people were shocked to read story after story of Catholic priests being removed from public ministry because of allegations of sexually abusing minors. Although the rate of abuse by Catholic priests was actually less than that of other professions, scandal emerged because of the high moral expectations people have for members of the clergy.[43]

When publicity on the clergy sex abuse crisis was at its height in the fall of 2002, the dissident Catholic homosexual group Dignity U.S.A. appealed to the U.S. Conference of Catholic Bishops "to stop blaming gay priests for the clergy sexual abuse scandal."[44] Dignity claimed that, "all credible evidence discounts any link between the molestation of children and homosexuality."[45]

Was there a link between homosexuality and the clerical abuse of minors? The April 2004 report by the John Jay College of Criminal Justice entitled *The Nature and Scope of the Problem of Sexual Abuse of Minors by Catholic Priests and Deacons in the United States* reveals that 80.9 % of the alleged victims of sexual abuse were

---

[41] Ibid., 10.

[42] Ibid.

[43] See *Sexual Abuse in Social Context: Catholic Clergy and Other Professionals: Special Report by the Catholic League for Religious and Civil Rights* (February 2004), available online at http://www.catholicleague.org/research/abuse_in_social_context.htm.

[44] Brian W. Clowes and David L. Sonnier, "Child Molestation by Homosexuals and Heterosexuals," *Homiletic & Pastoral Review* (May 2005), 44.

[45] Ibid.

males.[46] Only a small percentage of the alleged victims were prepubescent children under the age of 11. The vast majority of the cases involved minors between 11 and 17 years of age. In this latter age bracket, the alleged victims were 85.3 % male.[47] These statistics show that the clergy sex abuse crisis chiefly involved the homosexual abuse of adolescent boys, a reality more accurately described as "ephebophilia" than "pedophilia."[48] "Ephebophilia" is attraction to post-pubescent adolescents, whereas "pedophilia" is attraction to pre-pubescent children.

The revelation that homosexuality was involved in close to 81 % of the alleged cases of sexual abuse by Catholic clergy is sobering. It raises the question of the suitability of homosexual men for the priesthood, the diaconate, and the religious life. Even before the "clergy sex abuse crisis" of 2002, the Congregation for Catholic Education was studying the question of the relation of homosexuality to affective maturity and whether homosexual tendencies were a "counter-indication" of a priestly vocation. Moreover, as long ago as 1961, Congregation for Religious noted: "Advancement to religious vows and ordination should be barred to those who are afflicted with evil tendencies to homosexuality or pederasty, since for them the common life and priestly ministry would constitute serious dangers."[49] Apparently, many seminaries and religious congregations (for whom this directive was especially intended) did not follow this instruction, especially in the 1970s and 1980s. A prevailing view was that candidates for the priesthood were called

---

[46] See Table 4.3.1 of the John Jay Report, which can be found on the Web site of the U.S. Conference of Catholic Bishops, http://usccb.org/comm/mediarelations.shtml

[47] Cf. Table 3.5.4 of the John Jay report and Clowes and Sonnier, 48.

[48] Clowes and Sonnier, 47.

[49] Sacred Congregation for Religious, "Careful Selection and Training of Candidates for the States of Perfection and Sacred Orders," Feb. 2, 1961, no. 30.4; the entire text of this document can be found in Lincoln T. Bouscaren, S.J., and James O'Connor, S.J., *The Canon Law Digest*, vol. 5 (1961), Canon 973 [1917 *Code of Canon Law*], 452–486.

to a life of chaste celibacy, regardless as to whether they were homosexually or heterosexually oriented.[50]

After years of careful study, the Congregation for Catholic Education, on November 4, 2005, issued an *Instruction concerning the Criteria for the Discernment of Vocations with Regard to Persons with Homosexual Tendencies in View of Their Admission to the Seminary and to Holy Orders.*[51] The focus of this instruction is on how homosexual tendencies influence affective maturity and spiritual fatherhood, qualities needed in ordained ministers. After a review of basic Catholic moral doctrine on homosexuality, the Congregation states:

> In light of such teaching this Dicastery, in accord with the Congregation for Divine Worship and the Discipline of the Sacraments, believes it necessary to state clearly that the Church, while profoundly respecting the persons in question, cannot admit to the seminary or to holy orders those who practice homosexuality, present deep-seated homosexual tendencies or support the so-called "gay culture."[52]

The Congregation does not define "deep-seated homosexual tendencies," but it does offer some clarity by distinguishing such deep-seated inclinations from "homosexual tendencies that were only the expression of a transitory problem — for example, that of an adolescence not yet superseded."[53] Such "transitory" tendencies, however, "must be clearly overcome at least three years before ordination to the diaconate."[54]

---

[50] See John L. Allen, Jr., "Vatican Instruction bans most gays from priesthood; leaves final decision to bishops, superiors," *National Catholic Reporter* posted Nov. 23, 2005 online at http://www.nationalcatholicreporter.org/update/bn112305.htm

[51] An English translation of this document can be found on the Vatican Web site at http://www.vatican.va_curia/congregations/ccatheduc/documents/rc_con_ccatheduc_doc_20051104_istruzone_en.html.

[52] Congregation for Catholic Education, *Instruction concerning the Criteria for the Discernment of Vocations with Regard to Persons with Homosexual Tendencies in View of Their Admission to the Seminary and to Holy Orders* (Nov. 4, 2005), n. 2.

[53] Ibid.

[54] Ibid.

It seems clear that the Catholic Church wishes priests and deacons to be heterosexual men with a clear masculine identity. In this way, they can assume the role of "spiritual fatherhood" that is very much needed in the Church today. While homosexual people are to be treated with "respect and sensitivity,"[55] deep-seated homosexual tendencies are perceived as a symptom of an affective immaturity "that gravely hinders" those afflicted "from correctly relating to men and women."[56] There is a justifiable concern about "the negative consequences that can derive from the ordination of persons with deep-seated homosexual tendencies."[57]

Pastoral Care for Homosexuals in the Church

From what has already been said, it is evident that the Catholic Church believes that homosexual people must be accepted "with respect, compassion, and sensitivity" and that "every sign of unjust discrimination in their regard should be avoided."[58] The Church, however, is quite clear that homosexual acts can never be approved under any circumstances.[59] There can never be any "pastoral method or theory" that provides moral justification for homosexual acts.[60]

Unfortunately, some Catholic moralists, out of a distorted sense of compassion, have argued that homosexual acts can be morally acceptable if done within the context of a loving relationship. A Jesuit professor once wrote that: "Homosexual actions ... may be psychologically healthy ... and may even be a form of authentic Christian spirituality."[61] Many Catholic colleges and universities have endorsed

---

[55] Ibid; cf. CCC 2358.

[56] Congregation for Catholic Education, *Instruction concerning the Criteria for the Discernment of Vocations with Regard to Persons with Homosexual Tendencies,* n. 2.

[57] Ibid. For more detail on the relation of homosexuality to affective immaturity, see *Vocation sacerdotale et homosexualité* [Priestly vocation and homosexuality] by Monsignor Tony Anatrella, Oct. 2, 2006, found online on the Web site of inXL6, *le portail jeune de l'Église catholique en France* http://www.inxl6.org/article3103.php and Msgr. Anatrella's reflections on the Nov. 4, 2005 *Instruction* of the Congregation for Catholic Education published in the Italian edition of *L'Osservatore Romano* of Nov. 30, 2005.

[58] CCC 2358.

[59] Cf. CCC 2357 and *Persona Humana,* 8.

[60] *Persona Humana,* 8.

[61] Edward Vacek, S.J. "A Christian Homosexuality?" *America* (December 5, 1980), 683.

"gay and lesbian" student organizations that either ignore or completely reject Catholic moral teaching. Because of these trends, the Congregation for the Doctrine of the Faith, in 1986, urged bishops to be vigilant about pastoral programs for homosexuals that fail to defend Catholic moral teaching and do not protect Catholics with homosexual tendencies from the near occasions of sin.[62]

How should the Catholic Church provide authentic pastoral care to those suffering from deep-seated homosexual tendencies? Without intending to be exhaustive, I would propose the following guidelines:

1. Always be compassionate toward individuals, but firm on moral principles. True compassion requires looking out for the authentic good of others. We do not help homosexuals by giving them approval to engage in immoral actions. Because such acts are contrary to the natural law, they cannot ultimately serve the good of those who practice them. There might be an appearance of happiness and normalcy, but the violation of the moral law always carries with it negative consequences, either temporal or spiritual.

2. Encourage homosexuals to consider therapy. As the Catholic Medical Association has substantiated, many people with more or less strong homosexual tendencies have achieved complete or partial freedom from "homosexual behavior, fantasy or attraction."[63] One of the best resources in this regard is NARTH, the National Association for Research & Therapy of Homosexuality. The writings of Dr. Joseph J. Nicolosi, the President of NARTH, are especially valuable.[64]

---

[62] Congregation for the Doctrine of the Faith, *On the Pastoral Care of Homosexuals*, nos. 14–15.

[63] Catholic Medical Association, *Homosexuality and Hope*, no. 6.

[64] See Joseph J. Nicolosi, *Reparative Therapy of Male Homosexuality: A New Clinical Approach* (Lanham, MD: Jason Aronson Publishers, 2002). See also the Web site of NARTH (www.narth.com).

3. Encourage happiness through chastity. Even if reparative therapy is not successful in overcoming all homosexual attractions, chastity is always possible through God's grace. As the *Catechism* observes: "By the virtues of self-mastery that teach them inner freedom, at times by the support of disinterested friendship, by prayer and sacramental grace, [homosexuals][65] can and should gradually and resolutely approach Christian perfection."

4. Encourage constructive activities, especially in the service of others. There is a strong tendency toward narcissism in homosexuality. Single men and women who wish to be chaste need to become involved in the service of others. Helping out at a soup kitchen is a far more fulfilling pastime than going to "gay" nightclubs and bars. Creative hobbies such as music, writing, and painting are also worth developing, as long as they don't become sources of self-absorption. Sports and outdoor activities might also be valuable.

5. Encourage membership in support groups of prayer that are grounded in authentic Catholic morality and spirituality. Probably the best support group for Catholics struggling with homosexual tendencies is the apostolate COURAGE, founded by Fr. John Harvey, O.S.F.S., and Fr. Benedict J. Groeschel, C.F.R., in cooperation with some other priests and the late Terrence Cardinal Cooke of New York. There are now over 100 chapters of COURAGE grounded in the goals of chastity, prayer and dedication, fellowship, support, and good example.[66]

6. Discourage membership in "gay and lesbian" organizations that do not support Catholic morality or are ambiguous about it. Such organizations might provide an ephemeral sense of "belonging," but they are frequently

---

[65] CCC 2359.
[66] See http://courage.net/TheFiveGoals.html.

near occasions of sin. Catholic parishes, colleges, and universities that sponsor such groups are guilty of scandal. Catholics who join such organizations often get swept into the secular gay scene even if a veneer of religion is maintained.

7. Encourage the pursuit of holiness, which requires the cultivation of chastity. There can be no authentic growth in the knowledge and love of God if one is violating God's moral law. All Christians are summoned to "spiritual battle" because of the material effects of original sin and the temptations of the devil.[67] The Evil One has a way of keeping people in bondage through lustful habits and attitudes. Prayer, fasting, and other forms of asceticism are often needed to break free of the snares of the Evil One. Devotion to the Sacred Heart of Jesus and the Immaculate Heart of Mary are especially helpful in overcoming temptations.

8. Offer consolation and encouragement after failures. This is especially important for priests in the confessional. Many times, homosexuals wish to live chastely but they give in to temptations or lapse back into sinful habits. The desire to be chaste is the most important step toward achieving chastity. It is far better to be a sinner who recognizes sin than someone who has learned to rationalize immoral behavior. Our Lord came to call sinners and to offer them compassion, forgiveness, and hope.

---

[67] Cf. CCC 405.

CHAPTER EIGHT

FORNICATION AND COHABITATION

I remember teaching a high school religion class, and we were going over the Ten Commandments. When we got to the sixth commandment, one female student blurted out: "Well, adultery might be wrong, but the Bible says nothing about premarital sex!" This young woman obviously was mistaken, but I continue to be amazed at how many people have this impression. It is true, of course, that adultery is a different sin than fornication. As we saw in Chapter Three, the Greek New Testament uses one word for adultery (*moicheia*) and another for lewdness or fornication (*porneia*). Adultery occurs when there is marital infidelity: when sexual relations occur between two people "of whom at least one is married to another party."[1] Fornication, on the other hand, is the "carnal union between an unmarried man and an unmarried woman."[2] The Church teaches that fornication "is gravely contrary to the dignity of persons and of human sexuality which is naturally ordered to the good of the spouses and to the generation and education of children."[3]

The Old Testament condemns fornication. According to Deut 22:28–29, a man caught having sex with an unmarried woman would be required to marry her, pay a fine to her father, and promise never

---

[1] CCC 2380.
[2] CCC 2353.
[3] Ibid.

to divorce her. Virginity was highly prized in ancient Israel; so much so that a woman found not to be a virgin at the time of her marriage could be stoned to death (cf. Deut 22:20–21). We find further witness to the value of premarital virginity in Song of Solomon 8:4, where the daughters of Israel are admonished to "stir not up nor awaken love" before it is time.

The New Testament also condemns fornication. In Mt 15:19 and Mk 7:21, Jesus includes acts of fornication (*porneiai*) among the evils that come from the heart to defile a man. In 1 Cor 6:9, St. Paul includes fornicators (*pornoi*) among those who will not inherit the kingdom of God. In the same letter, he warns the Corinthians to avoid fornication because it is a sin against one's own body, which is the temple of the Holy Spirit (1 Cor 6:18–19). 1 Tim 1:10 lists fornicators among sinners like murderers and sodomites, who are "unholy and profane" and "contrary to sound doctrine." In a similar vein, Rev. 21:8 envisions fornicators among sinners like sorcerers, murderers, and idol-worshippers who share "in the lake that burns with fire and brimstone, which is the second death (cf. also Rev 22:15).

In spite of these stern warnings, some theologians have argued that, the *porneia* condemned by St. Paul referred to involvement with prostitutes and cannot be simply identified with those engaging in premarital intercourse."[4] Thus, some moralists argue that premarital sexual relations are not always wrong, but should be judged morally acceptable to the extent that they are "self-liberating, other-enriching, honest, faithful, self-serving, and joyous."[5] Others draw a distinction between premarital and "pre-ceremonial" sexual relations, the latter referring to relations between those who are engaged or intending to get married but have not yet made "the formal exchange of vows."[6] Other moralists argue that premarital intercourse is generally unacceptable unless an engaged couple expresses "the willingness and ability"

---

[4] Kosnik et al., 154.
[5] Ibid., 168.
[6] Ibid., 160.

to provide for the child who might be conceived from sexual union.[7]

All these attempts to justify premarital sexual relations run counter to the constant teaching of the Church "which asserts that sexual intercourse may only take place within marriage."[8] In its 1975 *Declaration on Certain Problems of Sexual Ethics*, the Congregation for the Doctrine of the Faith, teaches that,

> No matter how definite the intention of those who indulge in premarital sex, the fact is that such liaisons can scarcely ensure mutual sincerity and fidelity in a relationship between a man and a woman, nor especially can they protect it from inconstancy of desires or whim.[9]

The Congregation further notes that Jesus willed the stable union of marriage as the true context for "the two to become one body."[10] Furthermore, St. Paul "taught that if the unmarried or widows could not remain continent, they have no alternative but to marry."[11]

In addition to Scripture, human experience "teaches that love must be protected by the stability of marriage if sexual intercourse is really to meet the demands of its own finality and of human dignity."[12] Marriage serves the good of the spouses, and it provides future children with a stable environment of love in which they can best mature and flourish.

As noted earlier, the separation of sexual intimacy from marriage and children has had chaotic social effects. The so-called "sexual revolution" has led to the wider acceptance of promiscuity, abortion, and divorce. Family life suffers the most from irresponsible sexual behavior, and people are often depersonalized and wounded by sexual relations outside of marriage.

---

[7] Cf. Vincent Genovesi, S.J., *In Pursuit of Love: Catholic Morality and Human Sexuality* (Wilmington, DE: Michael Glazier, Inc., 1987), 170–171.

[8] *Persona Humana*, 7.

[9] Ibid.

[10] Ibid.; cf. Mt 19:4–6.

[11] *Persona Humana*, 7; cf. 1 Cor 7:9.

[12] *Persona Humana*, 7.

The Moral Evaluation of Cohabitation

According to published statistics, there were 500,000 Americans co-habitating in 1970. In 2004, the number had increased to more than 5 million.[13] Cohabitating refers to "living together in a sexual relationship without marriage."[14] People choose to cohabit for a variety of reasons. Sometimes, they do so for convenience, sometimes to consolidate resources and to save money. Some couples feel they are not yet ready for the commitment of marriage, and so they want a trial period to test their relationship.[15] In a pastoral letter on the subject, the Catholic bishops of Kansas summarize the reasons as follows: (1) testing period; (2) financial benefits; (3) convenience; (4) sexual need; (5) insecurity; (6) fear of commitment; (7) escape; (8) playing house; (9) no fear of pregnancy.[16]

There are some other sobering statistics: "Currently, 60% of all marriages are preceded by cohabitation;" "fewer than half of cohabiting unions end in marriage;" and marriages preceded by cohabitation are "46% more likely to end in divorce."[17] The statistics reveal one reality: those who cohabit are not increasing their chances of a happy and stable marriage. This follows because those who cohabit before marriage develop the mentality of imperma-nence with respect to relationships; this would be especially true

---

[13] These statistics are from David Popenoe and Barbara Whitehead, "The State of Our Unions: The Social Health of Marriage in America in 2005," *National Marriage Project* (New Brunswick, NJ: Rutgers University, 2005) 21–22; see http:marriage. rutgers.edu; these statistics are also cited on the Web site of the U.S. Conference of Catholic Bishops under the Secretariat for Family, Laity, Women and Youth, http://www. usccb.org/laity/marriage/cohabitation.shtml.

[14] U.S. Conference of Catholic Bishops under the Secretariat for Family, Laity, Women and Youth, http://www.usccb.org/laity/marriage/cohabitation.shtml.

[15] See Fr. Joseph M. Champlin, "Cohabitation before Marriage," *Catholic Update: June 2003* (Cincinnati, OH: St. Anthony Messenger Press, 2003).

[16] Cf. Kansas bishops, "Pastoral Letter on Cohabitation before Marriage," in *Origins* (June 4, 1998) (Washington, D.C., Catholic News Service, 1998), 39–44.

[17] These statistics are all cited on U.S. Conference of Catholic Bishops' Web site under the Secretariat for Family, Laity, Women and Youth, http://www.usccb.org/laity/marriage/cohabitation.shtml. Cohabitation, here, of course means living togeth-er and engaging in sexual activity. There are also cases where fornication regularly takes place even if separate residences are maintained. If these fornicating couples are considered, the percentage of couples who fornicate prior to marriage is certainly high-er than 60 %.

with those who lived together with several partners before marriage. Furthermore, those who choose to cohabit might have personality problems that will make marriage more difficult. They might have traits of insecurity, fear of commitment, or problems with infidelity. Indeed, cohabitating couples are twice as likely to have experienced an act of infidelity than married couples.[18]

These statistics provide sociological arguments against cohabitation, but Catholics should understand that sexual relations outside of marriage are morally wrong. Bishops and pastors often struggle with the problem of what to do with cohabitating couples who ask to get married in the Catholic Church. In and of itself, cohabitation is not an impediment to marriage. It is a sin that needs to be confessed, but it does not constitute *per se* an obstacle to getting married.

Some bishops, like Most Rev. John D'Arcy of the Diocese of Fort Wayne-South Bend, Indiana, have urged cohabitating couples to separate and abstain from sexual relations before marriage. If couples do not follow this advice, then pastors might either postpone the wedding or arrange for a small, quiet service.[19] Other pastors try to follow a "don't ask, don't tell" policy when it comes to couples who might be cohabitating. This, though, would be a failure to properly prepare the couple for the sacrament of marriage and a life in obedience to God's moral law.

In the end, the priest or deacon who witnesses a marriage should have moral certitude that the bride and groom are prepared to pursue the proper ends of the sacrament. Couples who cohabit and manifest no compunction might need to be asked some pointed questions as to why they wish to be married in the Catholic Church. If they are so willing to flaunt the moral law before marriage, how can they be expected to follow the moral law after they get married? In such cases, a postponement of the marriage might

---

[18] Cf. Judith Treas and Deidre Giesen, "Sexual Infidelity among Married and Cohabitating Americans," *Journal of Marriage and the Family*, vol. 62, no. 1 (February 2000), 48–60.

[19] Cf. Champlin, "Cohabitation before Marriage."

be in order until the couple manifests a greater commitment to and understanding of the sacrament. On the other hand, a priest or deacon counseling a cohabitating couple could use the marriage preparation period as an opportunity to evangelize and catechize. If sufficient progress has been made, then the ordained minister can precede with the plans to witness the marriage.

Dating and Sexual Activity

In today's highly erotic culture, living chastely as a single person is often challenging. We have already touched upon the need for God's grace to overcome temptations, but what guidance should be given to teenagers and young adults who are dating? The best guidance is the encouragement of chaste friendships. To get to know someone takes time. If a relationship develops around various forms of sexual exploration, a bond can form around mutual needs for sexual gratification rather than a true respect for the other. Many single people date with sexual needs in mind. The person of the opposite sex becomes a means to an end. Sometimes the exploitation is mutual. Other times, one of the parties, often the man, is focused chiefly on sexual enjoyment, while the other partner goes along with the sexual activity in pursuit of love. The end result is often tragic and painful.

From a Catholic perspective, dating with sexual gratification in mind is clearly immoral. Sometimes, dating couples believe they are following the moral law as long as they avoid sexual intercourse. They, therefore, engage in heavy kissing, intimate touching, mutual masturbation, and, sometimes, oral sex. Regarding such activities, Christopher West offers this sound advice:

> Similarly, physical behaviors that aim to arouse the body in preparation for intercourse (fondling each other's genitals or breasts, and even some kinds of extended kissing and embracing) are not appropriate expressions of affection for the unmarried. When there is simply no moral possibility of consummated love, it is, in fact, unloving to arouse someone

to the point of physical craving for intercourse. If we must talk about physical lines in order to keep our hearts honest, we can say this: if either the man or the woman is brought to the verge of climax, or has reached climax, or is aroused to the point of being tempted to masturbate, such a couple "crossed the line" *a long time before* and is in serious need of examining their hearts and their motives.[20]

To be sure, men and women (in their 20s and older) who are dating with the possibility of marriage in mind will begin to show signs of physical affection. Various forms of kissing and embracing each other can be morally acceptable as long as these do not lead to the point at which the drive for climax takes over. Those who are dating must learn to set limits on their signs of affection, and they need to communicate openly about this. When the two are clear about their desire to remain chaste, things go much more easily. If, however, a dating couple crosses the line of propriety on one occasion, it becomes easier to do so again. Soon, patterns of mutual arousal can become the norm and chastity becomes very difficult to maintain.

Catholic men and women who are dating should learn to spend time together before the Blessed Sacrament, read Scripture, or pray the Rosary together. If God is calling them to marriage, they should begin to develop mutual habits of prayer and devotion. Not only will such practices help them maintain chastity in their relationship, they will also help them grow more deeply in love with the Lord as they grow in love for each other.

Reasons against Premarital Sex

From what has already been said, it is clear that both Scripture and Catholic moral doctrine condemn premarital sexual relations. The reasons why sexual relations prior to marriage are harmful and immoral can be summarized as follows:

---

[20] Christopher West, *Good News about Sex and Marriage*, Revised Edition (Cincinnati, OH: Servant Books, 2004), 76; see also Mary Beth Bonacci, *Real Love: Mary Beth Bonacci Answers Your Questions on Dating, Marriage and the Real Meaning of Sex* (San Francisco: Ignatius Press, 1996), especially pp. 186-196.

1. Such sexual relations usually are not open to having children, and, therefore, they go against the procreative end of the conjugal act. Many who engage in such sexual activity use contraception, which shows no reverence for the natural ordination of the sexual act. When a child is conceived, abortion is often considered as an option, so one wrongdoing leads to another. Other times, the pregnancy will prompt the parents to get married, but without adequate preparation. When the parents don't get married, the child is brought into the world deprived of the stable environment that marriage is meant to provide. Many people are under the impression that the widespread availability of contraception will help decrease unwanted pregnancies and recourse to abortion. There is, however, much evidence showing a connection between contraception and abortion.[21]

2. Sexual relations prior to marriage psychologically sever the link between marriage and the conjugal act. Those who engage in sexual intercourse prior to marriage easily lose the sense that conjugal intimacy is a sign of permanent, committed love.

3. Habitual sexual intimacy by unmarried couples hinders the development of true love, mutual respect, and genuine knowledge of each other. Because the pleasure of sexual intimacy is so powerful, couples can grow to depend on each other for mutual sexual satisfaction rather than grow in the appreciation of each other as persons. The dangers of mutual exploitation are especially strong, often leading to deep psychological wounds and/or a hardening of hearts.

4. Sexual intercourse is linked to "the language of the body." Conjugal intimacy is meant to embody love that is fully

---

[21] See Janet E. Smith, "The Connection between Contraception and Abortion," *Homiletic and Pastoral Review* (April 1993), 10–18.

[22] Cf. Paul VI, *Humanae Vitae*, 9.

human, total, exclusive, and fruitful.[22] When couples engage in sexual intercourse outside of marriage, dishonesty is present because they do not really intend the true meaning of the act that physically unites them. They may find themselves lying to each other in many ways.

5. Premarital sexual relations are linked to higher divorce rates (as seen earlier). One reason for this is that those who cohabit before marriage have fears of making permanent commitments, and such fears make lasting commitments all the more difficult. Because sexual intimacy for them can take place *without* marriage, sexual intimacy *within* marriage no longer is understood as a sign of permanent love.

6. Those who fornicate and cohabit before marriage manifest a willingness to violate the moral law of God. If they are willing to violate God's law *before* marriage, it is more likely that they will violate God's law *after* marriage. Fidelity to God's law, however, is essential for marital happiness and stability.

7. Sexual intercourse prior to marriage injures one's relationship with God and jeopardizes the life of grace. Scripture teaches that fornicators will not inherit the kingdom of God.[23]

---

[23] Cf. 1 Cor 6:9; Gal 5:19; Rev 22:15.

CHAPTER NINE

MARITAL CHASTITY

The Catholic Church teaches that all of us are called to chastity according to our state of life. For those who are married, this means making use of the conjugal act in accordance with the divine and natural law as interpreted by the Church. Some people have the misconception that marriage provides a *carte blanche* to engage in any type of sexual activity short of rape. Husbands and wives, however, must make proper use of the great gift of sexual intimacy. They must not regard each other as objects for sexual gratification but as persons united in a "partnership of the whole of life."[1]

As we have seen, Pope Paul VI beautifully summarized the four "characteristic marks and demands of conjugal love."[2] Such intimate acts are: (1) fully human; (2) total; (3) faithful and exclusive until death; and (4) fruitful or fecund, that is, ordered to the gift of children, who are the "supreme gift of marriage."[3] Behind this teaching is the recognition of the intrinsic connection, willed by God, between the unitive and procreative meanings of the conjugal act.[4] This intrinsic connection is "inscribed into the very being of man and woman"[5] and inscribed into the very language of the marital act. As a result of this intrinsic connection, it is necessary "that each and every marriage act remain ordered *per se* to the procreation of human life."[6]

---

[1] *Code of Canon Law* [1983], canon 1055.1.
[2] Paul VI, *Humanae Vitae*, 9.
[3] Cf. Ibid., and *Gaudium et Spes*, 50.
[4] Cf. Paul VI, *Humanae Vitae*, 12.
[5] Ibid.
[6] Ibid., 11; cf. CCC 2366.

To deliberately separate the conjugal act from its procreative meaning is to act against the natural law, the order of right reason established by the Creator.[7] As we saw in our discussion of the "theology of the body," the conjugal act, by its very nature, communicates total self-giving. When contraception is used, however, this language of "total reciprocal self-giving" is distorted by "an objectively contradictory language, namely that of not giving oneself totally to the other."[8]

The Church recognizes that there might be reasons for spacing offspring that are "defensible," "weighty," and "worthy."[9] In such cases, "the Church teaches that it is then licit to take into account the natural rhythms immanent in the generative functions, for the use of marriage in the infecund periods only."[10] In 1968, when *Humanae Vitae* was issued, this was understood as the "rhythm method" of regulating birth. But, since then, there has been the development of methods of natural family planning (NFP) that are far more accurate than the older "rhythm" methods for regulating birth. One recent study showed that NFP has a 99 % success rate in avoiding pregnancy.[11] Every Catholic diocese and (ideally) every Catholic parish should provide opportunities for training in methods of natural family planning. Accurate information about NFP should be part of every marriage preparation class.[12]

Married couples, of course, can use the fertility awareness derived from NFP to help achieve pregnancy. They may also use NFP to avoid pregnancy if they have serious, just, or plausible reasons for avoiding pregnancy at certain times within their marriage. In

---

[7] Cf. CCC 1956.

[8] John Paul II, *Familiaris Consortio*, 32.

[9] Cf. *Humnae Vitae*, 16.

[10] Ibid.

[11] Shao-Zhen Quian, "China Successfully Launching Billings Ovulation Method," *Bulletin of the Ovulation Method Research and Reference Centre of Australia* 30, 2 (June 2003), 11, 12.

[12] Information about Natural Family Planning can be obtained from the Paul VI Institute in Omaha, NE; (popepaul@popepaulvi.com) from a Web site maintained by John and Sheila Kippley (www.NFPandmore.org) and from the Natural Family Planning Office of the U.S. Conference of Catholic Bishops (NFP@usccb.org), which provides a listing of diocesan NFP coordinators. See also resources put out by Janet E. Smith on the moral use of NFP and "Contraception: Why Not?" located on www.mycatholicfaith.org.

making the decision to avoid pregnancy at a particular time, the couple has "a duty to make certain that their desire is not motivated by selfishness but is in conformity with the generosity appropriate to responsible parenthood."[13] The moral use of NFP, however, should not be understood as the moral equivalent of contraception. Because it relies upon periodic continence, NFP "is in conformity with the objective criteria of morality."[14] NFP respects the language of the body, and it never separates the unitive and procreative meanings of any given conjugal act. Moreover, NFP requires virtue, self-control, and mutual communication between the spouses. This is why it serves to increase rather than diminish marital love. While the divorce rate for couples that use contraception is close to 50%, the divorce rate among those who use NFP is "almost negligible."[15]

In *Humanae Vitae*, Pope Paul VI predicted that the widespread use of contraception would lead to four grave consequences: (1) It would open the way to conjugal infidelity and other forms of sexual immorality; (2) it would lead to widespread disrespect for women and their physical and psychological well-being; (3) it would become a dangerous weapon in the hands of public authority; and (4) it would give human beings the impression that we have limitless dominion over our bodies.[16] There are good reasons for believing that all four of these predications have come true.[17] Contraception has not led to better marriages and family life. On the contrary, it has injured them.

It is well known that many Catholics do not follow the Church's teaching regarding contraception.[18] This, though, does not mean

---

[13] CCC 2368.

[14] Ibid., 2370.

[15] Cf. Janet E. Smith, "Paul VI as Prophet," in Janet E. Smith, ed. *Why Humanae Vitae Was Right: A Reader* (San Francisco: Ignatius Press, 1993), 526; see also Christopher West, *Good News About Sex and Marriage* (2004), 131.

[16] Paul VI, *Humanae Vitae*, 17; see also William E. May, "*Humanae Vitae* at 40: Abundant Contemporary Literature from the Social Sciences Confirms Paul VI's Warnings about Contraception," *The Catholic World Report* (July 2008): 40-46.

[17] Cf. Janet E. Smith, "Paul VI as Prophet," 521–528.

[18] According to a 1994 *New York Times*/CBS poll as many as 98 % of Catholics 19–29 years of age practice artificial birth control; and 92 % of those 30–44; cited in John E. Thiel, "Tradition and Reasoning: A Nonfoundationalist Perspective," *Theological Studies* 56 (Dec., 1995) 627–651; footnote 8.

the teaching is wrong. Many Catholics have not been properly instructed on this matter, and many are not even aware of NFP. The failure to accept the teaching of *Humanae Vitae* also is connected with decline in Mass attendance and other signs of Catholic infidelity.[19] As noted earlier, the widespread use of contraception has not had a positive influence on marriages and family life, and couples who follow the Church's teaching have happier and more stable marriages.

The Catholic Church's teaching against contraception was the standard Christian teaching until the change in Anglican teaching on the subject in 1930.[20] For centuries, Christians understood the Bible as condemning artificial birth control.[21] Most prominent among the biblical reasons for resisting contraception is the story of Onan, who is killed by the Lord for refusing to have children with his wife (his brother's widow) and spilling his seed on the ground.[22] The Catholic Magisterium in the 1800s and early 1900s had numerous interventions concerning the "onanistic use of marriage" (*De usu onanistico matrimonii*), that is the deliberate interruption of the marital act and the spilling of the seed outside of the vagina.[23] Thus, what Paul VI taught in *Humanae Vitae* was the long-standing teaching of the Church, firmly rooted in Scripture and Tradition.

Connected with the Church's teaching against contraception is her teaching against *direct sterilization*. Although it is morally acceptable to accept sterilization as an indirect effect of a needed operation (e.g., a hysterectomy), the Congregation for the Doctrine of the Faith in 1975 made it clear that "any sterilization whose sole, immediate effect, of itself, that is, of its own nature and con-

---

[19] Cf. John F. Kippley, *Sex and the Marriage Covenant: A Basis for Morality*, Second Edition (San Francisco: Ignatius Press, 2005), 191.

[20] Ibid., 152.

[21] Cf. Charles Provan, *The Bible and Birth Control* (Monongahela, PA: Zimmer Printing, 1989).

[22] Cf. Gen 38:6–9.

[23] Cf. Denz.-H, 2715; 2758–2760; 2791–2793; 2795; 3185–3187; 3634; 3638–3640.

dition, is to render the generative faculty incapable of procreation ... is absolutely forbidden."[24] This would apply to direct sterilization for men as well as women.

Marital chastity, as we have seen, is violated by contraception and direct sterilization, and some couples regret being sterilized. Whether there is a moral obligation to seek reversals of such sterilizations is a matter of debate among Catholic theologians.[25] Even if it is not obligatory, couples should seriously consider pursuing sterilization reversals if the cost is not prohibitive. In this way, they can better integrate the unitive and procreative meanings of the conjugal act.

Other Questions Related to Marital Chastity

Needless to say, *direct abortion* is forbidden. Abortion actually is a violation of the fifth commandment ("thou shalt not kill") rather than the sixth commandment.[26] Sadly, it has become a method of birth control in certain contexts. The tragedy of abortion, though, shows that sexual sins can lead to other sins. Irresponsible sexual behavior can lead to the direct killing of innocent human life by way of abortion.[27] The Catholic Church, relying on sound medical science and anthropology, teaches that from the time of conception, that is, from the time the zygote is formed, there is the life of a new human being who is "to be respected and treated as a person."[28] Abortion, therefore, involves the direct killing of an innocent human being. As the constant teaching of the ordinary and universal Magisterium, the condemnation of abortion must be considered a definitive, and, therefore, infallible, teaching of the Church.[29] The Church, since the first century, has consistently condemned

---

[24] CDF, *Haec Sacra Congregatio*, March 13, 1975, 1; Denz.-H, 4560.
[25] Janet E. Smith and Christopher Kaczor, *Life Issues, Medical Choices: Questions and Answers for Catholics* (Cincinnati, OH: Servant Books, 2007), 95–97.
[26] Cf. CCC 2270–2272.
[27] See John Paul II, *Evangelium Vitae*, 13, where he notes that "contraception and abortion are often closely connected, as fruits of the same tree."
[28] Cf. CDF, *Donum Vitae*, I, 1.
[29] Cf. John Paul II, *Evangelium Vitae* [1995], no. 62.

"the moral evil of every procured abortion."[30] This is a teaching that "has not changed and remains unchangeable."[31]

Adultery refers to sexual relations with someone other than one's spouse or sexual relations with someone else's spouse. It is a direct offense to marital chastity. It not only offends marital chastity, it also involves a grave injustice to one's spouse.[32] Sacred Scripture clearly and consistently condemns adultery.[33] Jesus condemned not only the act of adultery but lustful thoughts that involve adultery of the heart.[34] A husband who truly loves his wife and a wife who truly loves her husband will avoid any temptations toward adultery. There can be no doubt that adultery is a grave sin that can deprive a person of the kingdom of God.[35]

In addition to contraception, sterilization, abortion, and adultery, there are other offenses against marital chastity that should be mentioned. Some couples make use of *pornography* as sexual stimulation within marriage. Such a practice, however, is a grave violation of marital chastity. Pornography, by its very nature, offends against human dignity and has no place within a chaste marriage.[36]

Another question often raised is that of *oral sex*. In traditional manuals of moral theology, oral sex was understood as the improper use of a *vas indebitum* (unworthy receptacle) and linked with sodomy.[37] This prohibition against oral sex, however, seems to assume that the mouth will be used as a receptacle for the semen. Some contemporary Catholic moralists have raised the question whether oral stimulation of the genitals can be morally accepted as part of "foreplay" leading up to conjugal union. Catholic authors such as Kippley and West believe oral sex (fellatio or cunnilingus) is moral-

---

[30] CCC 2271.
[31] Ibid.
[32] Cf. CCC 2381.
[33] Cf. Ex 2020:14; Deut 5:18; Mk 7:22.
[34] Mt 5:28.
[35] Cf. 1 Cor 6:9.
[36] Cf. CCC 2354.
[37] Cf. Marcellinus Zalba, *Theologiae Moralis Summa* II (Madrid: Biblioeteca de Autores Cristianos, 1957), no. 393, p.165. Zalba refers to the "abuse of the mouth" (*abusus oris*) by the Latin term, *irrumatio*.

ly permitted as part of foreplay, though "it must never be forced upon an unwilling spouse."[38] Both authors also agree that oral sex should not be used as an alternative to marital intercourse but only as a possible prelude. In a similar manner, Ford and Kelly refrain from condemning oral-genital foreplay altogether. Instead, they suggest that such acts be evaluated on an individual basis according to the principles of conjugal chastity and "Christian self-restraint."[39]

Usually, men are more interested in oral-genital stimulation than women, but some women are also interested in such stimulation when performed on them. Some wives might go along with oral-genital forms of foreplay to please their husbands, but there should be open and honest communication in this regard. The rules of justice and charity must always have priority, and it would be unfair for one spouse to seek forms of stimulation the other finds unpleasant.

West and Kippley both discuss the possibility of *anal-genital stimulation* as a form of foreplay. Although West does not believe it can be ruled out objectively, he finds it very questionable from the viewpoints of hygiene and subjective marital sensitivity.[40] Kippley, in a similar fashion, believes that "anal penetration" as foreplay "would be so unsanitary that it is difficult to imagine any possible moral use."[41]

Mutual masturbation is another issue that relates to marital chastity. Some couples believe they are following Church teaching as long as they refrain from contraceptive devices. Thus, they will substitute mutual masturbation for intercourse on days when conception is likely. From a Catholic perspective, however, deliberate mutual masturbation, entirely removed from the context of conjugal intercourse, "falls under the same condemnation as solitary masturbation."[42] Lawler, Boyle, and May believe that "the person-uniting

---

[38] Kippley, 45; cf. West, 92–93.
[39] Ford and Kelly, 228–229.
[40] Cf. West, 93–94.
[41] Kippley, 46.
[42] Ibid.

and procreative aspects of sexual activity" are still trivialized "in masturbation between spouses," even though there is a mutual rather than solitary dimension.[43] In mutual masturbation, the focus usually is on the pleasure of orgasm rather than on the true goods associated with marital love.[44] To this can be added the observation of the Congregation for the Doctrine of the Faith that "the deliberate use of the sexual faculty outside normal conjugal relations essentially contradicts the finality of the faculty."[45] In the older manuals, mutual masturbation was addressed under the category of "pollution" and was condemned if ejaculation or orgasm, apart from intercourse, was deliberately intended.[46]

From a pastoral perspective, it should be understood that involuntary ejaculations might occur during intimate foreplay. It might also happen that one or both spouses will, without planning, achieve sexual climax prior to intercourse, thereby diminishing the motivation for sexual union. In such cases, there would not seem to be an obligation to complete sexual intercourse. Couples, however, that habitually engage in acts likely to lead to climax (outside of sexual union) should ask themselves whether they actually intend such acts as substitutions for intercourse. In cases of doubt, it might be advisable to seek moral counsel from a priest in confession.[47]

Another issue that needs to be addressed is whether it is permitted for a husband to help his wife achieve orgasm after sexual intercourse if she was not able to achieve one during the act of union. Ford and Kelly suggest that this is only permitted if the orgasm is "in immediate conjunction with the marriage act, so that, morally speaking, it is part of the marriage act."[48] For Kippley, there is no moral problem with a husband assisting his wife "by way of man-

---

[43] Lawler et al., 181.
[44] Cf. ibid.
[45] CDF, *Persona Humana*, 9.
[46] Cf. Zalba, nos. 369–392, pp. 155–164.
[47] Cf. also Ford and Kelly, p. 197, where a distinction is made between occasional unintended orgasms and those that occur frequently due to imprudence or even recklessness.
[48] Ford and Kelly, 212.

ual-clitoral stimulation to achieve orgasm after his." Indeed, he believes this might even be "an act of marital virtue to assist her toward relief and full satisfaction." For him, all of this can be considered "part of one moral act of marital relations."[49]

When all is said and done, marital chastity hinges on the principles of charity, justice, and observance of the moral law. The intrinsic connection between the unitive and procreative meanings of the conjugal act must never be hindered, even if procreation is impossible. Conjugal relations always remain procreative in "type" even if, due to biological reasons, they will not be procreative in "effect." God has linked the act of marital union with the awesome reality of procreation. What God has joined together, human beings must not separate.

---

[49] Kippley, 46.

CHAPTER TEN

THE MAGISTERIUM, CONSCIENCE, AND THE QUESTION OF DISSENT

The topic of sexual morality touches us where we are most vulnerable. The desire for love and intimacy is so strong that many people feel a sense of entitlement to seek sexual fulfillment according to their own standards of what is right and wrong. There is also the cultural factor. Catholic sexual morality seems unrealistic and outdated to many people today, and they wonder whether the Church will ever wake up to reality and catch up with the times.

In point of fact, I believe there has been a persistent effort in many Catholic circles to accommodate traditional sexual morality to the needs of the day. The results, though, have not been too happy. At least since the late 1960s, many influential Catholic theologians have been calling for a revision of Catholic sexual morality. In many ways, these theologians wish the Catholic Church to go the way of some "progressive" Protestant groups that have embraced not only contraception but also divorce and remarriage, abortion, and the blessing of homosexual unions.[1]

In the late 1960s, the chief issue was contraception, and many Catholic theologians hoped for a change in the Church's position. When Pope Paul VI reaffirmed the traditional Catholic doctrine in *Humanae Vitae* in 1968, the next tactic was to claim a right to "responsible dissent" from "official" Catholic moral teaching. At the

---

[1] For example, in July 2005, the rights of couples to get married regardless of gender was affirmed by 80% of the delegates at the General Synod of the United Church of Christ; cf. http://www.lifesitesnews.com/1dn/2005/jul/05070501.html.

center of this controversy was Fr. Charles Curran, a priest of the Diocese of Rochester, New York, and a member of the theology faculty at the Catholic University of America (CUA). In 1967, the Board of Trustees at CUA voted to terminate the contract of Fr. Curran. A campus-wide public protest ensued, and many students and professors refused to go to class until the university reversed its decision on Fr. Curran. Several leading archbishops, including Lawrence Shehan of Baltimore and Cardinal Cushing of Boston, intervened on behalf of Curran.[2] Cardinal O'Boyle of Washington eventually decided to reinstate Fr. Curran as a member of the faculty.

The affair catapulted Curran into the public limelight. In 1968, after the release of *Humanae Vitae*, he emerged as the most visible dissenting voice against the encyclical. In 1969, he was voted President of the Catholic Theological Society of America (CTSA). Under his leadership, the CTSA became a vehicle for public dissent from Magisterial teachings. Then, in 1977, a study authorized by the CTSA entitled *Human Sexuality: New Directions in American Catholic Thought* was released.[3] It received criticism from both the U.S Bishops' Committee on Doctrine and the Congregation for the Doctrine of Faith for its challenge to traditional Catholic teachings against contraception, premarital sex, masturbation, and homosexual acts.

The damage, though, had been done. Moral theologians became even more outspoken in their dissent. As noted earlier, a Jesuit priest published an article in 1980 suggesting that "homosexual actions … may be psychologically healthy … and may even be a form of authentic Christian spirituality."[4] Another theology profes-

---

[2] Larry Witham, *Curran vs. Catholic University: A Study of Authority and Freedom in Conflict* (Riverdale, MD: Edington-Rand, Inc., 1991), 24.

[3] Kosnik et al. (cited earlier). An overview of magisterial and theological reactions to the Kosnick book as well as to the 1975 declaration *Persona Humana* of the CDF can be found in Ralph J. Tapia, "Human Sexuality: The Magisterium and the Moral Theologians," *Thought*, vol. 54, no. 215 (December 1979), 405-418. This review contains much useful information, but Msgr. Tapia, the author, seems to have some sympathy for the methodology and conclusions of Kosnick et al.

[4] Edward Vacek, S.J., "A Christian Homosexuality?," *America* (December 5, 1980), 683.

sor asked whether "genital sexual relationships" for single people "might not only be permissible but even beneficial."[5]

The Magisterium during this time was not silent. In 1975, the Congregation for the Doctrine of the Faith (CDF) issued a *Declaration on Certain Questions Concerning Sexual Ethics (Persona Humana)* that reaffirmed traditional Catholic morality on premarital sex, masturbation, and some other issues. In 1986, the CDF published a letter to Catholic bishops, *On the Pastoral Care of Homosexual Persons*, which underscored the immorality of homosexual acts while at the same time defending the dignity of people with homosexual tendencies. Also in 1986, the CDF removed the canonical mission of Fr. Curran to teach theology in the name of the Church. In the final analysis, he was censured not merely for his stance against *Humanae Vitae* but also for his dissident teachings on abortion, euthanasia, masturbation, homosexual acts, and the indissolubility of marriage.[6]

With regard to sexual morality, the Magisterium of the Church has been very consistent in affirming certain positions. Many theologians, on the other hand, have looked upon the Church's sexual doctrines as open to question and debate. Where do the faithful fit into the equation in all this?

The alleged "right to dissent" on sexual morality has been based on flawed theology and a misrepresentation of Vatican II. Fr. Curran claimed that he was not disagreeing with any infallible teachings and, therefore, his dissent was loyal and responsible. In point of fact, Curran's position on divorce and remarriage challenged the infallible teaching of the Council of Trent on the indissolubility of marriage.[7] In reality, however, his appeal to an alleged right to public dissent from authentic Magisterial teachings has no foundation in the documents of Vatican II or any subsequent document of the Holy See.

---

[5] Francine Cardman *Spirituality Today*, vol. 34, no. 4 (Winter 1983), 311.
[6] Cf. *Origins*, vol. 15. no. 41 (Nov. 27, 1986), 670.
[7] Cf. Denz.-H., 1805–1807.

Curran claims that *Humanae Vitae* is not infallible and, therefore, public dissent against it is permitted. By way of response, it should first be noted that a strong case can be made that the teaching of *Humanae Vitae* is infallible by virtue of the ordinary and universal Magisterium.[8] But even if the teaching is not infallible, it would still be an expression of the ordinary papal Magisterium. *Lumen Gentium*, 25, of Vatican II, has this to say about how the faithful are to receive pronouncements of the ordinary papal Magisterium:

> Certainly, this religious submission of will and intellect (*religiosum voluntatis et intellectus obsequium*) must be shown in a special manner to the authentic magisterium of the Roman Pontiff even when he is not speaking *ex cathedra*: namely, in such a way that his supreme teaching authority is acknowledged with reverence, and that the judgments expressed by him are sincerely adhered to according to his manifest mind and will; these are especially revealed by the character of the documents (*indole documentorum*), by the frequent repetition of the same doctrine, or by the manner of speaking.[9]

At the very least, the teaching of *Humanae Vitae* is deserving of the "religious submission of will and intellect" described here. Quite possibly, it merits an even higher level of assent (if it expresses the teaching of the ordinary and universal Magisterium). All of this touches on the issue of the levels of assent owed to Magisterial teachings. What type of assent is owed to the moral doctrines of the Church concerning human sexuality?

In 1989, the Congregation for the Doctrine of the Faith issued a *Profession of Faith* that expresses three levels of assent. The first and

---

[8] Cf. Kippley, 152–171, and John C. Ford, S.J., and Germain Grisez, "Contraception and the Infallibility of the Ordinary Magisterium," *Theological Studies* 39:2 (June 1978), 258–312.

[9] My translation of the Latin, which more or less follows the N.C.W.C. translation used in the Daughters of St. Paul edition of *Lumen Gentium* as well the Italian translation found in Denzinger-Hünermann 37th ed. (Bologna: Edizioni Dehoniane, 1995), 4149.

highest level is that of firm faith in "each and everything contained in the Symbol of faith"[10] (the Nicene-Constantinopolitan Creed). This highest level of assent also includes "each and everything contained in the Word of God, whether written or handed down in tradition, which the Church, either by a solemn judgment or by the ordinary and universal Magisterium, sets forth to be believed as divinely revealed."[11] These teachings are to be believed with the assent of faith because they are "based directly on the authority of the Word of God."[12] Examples of such teachings would be the divinity of Christ, the Marian dogmas of the Immaculate Conception and the Assumption, and the real and substantial presence of Christ in the Eucharist.[13]

The second level of assent states: "I also firmly accept and hold each and everything definitively proposed by the Church regarding teachings on faith and morals."[14] Such definitive teachings demand "full and irrevocable assent" based on "faith in the Holy Spirit's assistance to the Magisterium."[15] Included among these definitive teachings are: "the illicitness of prostitution and of fornication."[16]

The third level of assent is expressed by this passage of the *Profession of Faith*: "Moreover, I adhere with religious submission of will and intellect to the teachings which either the Roman Pontiff or the College of Bishops enunciate when they exercise their authentic Magisterium even if they do not intend to proclaim these teachings by a definitive act."[17] In its *Commentary*, the CDF does not offer any concrete examples of teachings associated with this third level of assent, but it's safe to say that Magisterial teachings that do not fall under the first two levels of assent fall under this third.

---

[10] John Paul II, Apostolic Letter *Motu Proprio, Ad Tuendam Fidem* (Boston: Pauline Books & Media, 1998): Appendix A: Profession of Faith, 26.

[11] Ibid, 27.

[12] See the CDF's "Commentary on the Concluding Formula of the '*Professio Fidei*,'" no. 8 that appears after *Ad Tuendam Fidem* in ibid., 18.

[13] CDF, *Commentary*, no. 11; ibid., 20–21.

[14] *Profession*, ibid., 27.

[15] CDF, *Commentary*, no. 8; ibid., 18.

[16] Ibid., no. 11; 22.

[17] *Profession*, ibid., 27.

Where do the teachings of the Church concerned with sexual morality fit in? At the very least, they fall under the third level of assent in which case we are to adhere to them "with religious submission of will and intellect." The examples given by the CDF for the first two levels are not exhaustive. Thus, we could argue that the Church's condemnations of contraception, masturbation, and homosexual acts are definitive judgments of the ordinary and universal Magisterium. As such, they would require definitive assent, which is "full and irrevocable." The important thing to keep in mind is that faithful Catholics are to adhere to the moral teachings of the Magisterium on sexual matters. Most of these teachings have a firm grounding in Sacred Scripture, and they have been consistently taught by the Magisterium of the Church down through the centuries.

Unfortunately, many Catholics are under the impression that if a doctrine is not taught with the full weight of Magisterial authority, it is open to question and debate. The Church, however, recognizes that "divine assistance is also given to the successors of the apostles teaching in communion with the successor of Peter and, in a particular way, to the Roman Pontiff as Pastor of the whole Church, when exercising their ordinary Magisterium."[18] Those who teach in the name of the Church have a special obligation to present Catholic doctrines with "integrity and full accuracy."[19] If a particular theologian experiences difficulty with a particular teaching, he or she "has the duty to make known to the Magisterial authorities the problems raised by the teaching in itself, in the arguments proposed to justify it, or even in the manner in which it is presented."[20]

At no point, though, should a theologian resort to public dissent from the teachings of the Church. Such open dissent causes "serious harm" to the faithful and to the Church as a whole.[21]

---

[18] Congregation for the Doctrine of the Faith, *The Ecclesial Vocation of the Theologian, Donum Veritatis* (1990), no. 17.

[19] Ibid., no. 22.

[20] Ibid., no. 30.

[21] Cf. ibid., no. 32.

Dissent can take on different forms. At times, it is inspired by philosophical liberalism, relativism, and inspiration from political society.[22] At times, it has recourse to the mass media for attention.[23] Especially in matters of sexual morality, dissent can be a very destructive force. It serves to break down the trust the faithful should have in their bishops who, when united with the Roman Pontiff, "speak in the name of Christ."[24] Moreover, it is somewhat arrogant to think that one has greater insight into matters of sexual morality than the college of bishops who "are to be respected by all as witnesses to divine and Catholic truth."[25]

Vatican II recognized the importance of conscience, "that secret core and sanctuary" where we are alone with God whose voice echoes in our depths.[26] Many people, however, erroneously think of conscience as the source of the moral law. Conscience, though, is the interior means by which we perceive the law of God and apply it in the concrete circumstances of life. The moral law comes from God, either through divine revelation or the natural law. It does not come from any human source. Conscience, therefore, must "always bear witness to the authority of truth in reference to the supreme Good," that is, God.[27]

The God who speaks to us in the depths of our conscience is the same God who guides the Magisterium of the Church. It is for this reason that in forming our consciences we must diligently attend to "sacred and certain teaching of the Church" because "the Catholic Church is by the will of Christ the teacher of truth."[28]

In matters of sexual morality, Catholics should learn to trust in the wisdom of the Church. We should cultivate a spirit of docility and humility to the teaching authority of the bishops united with the Pope. Even if we fail, we should know that the moral

---

[22] Cf. ibid., nos. 32–34.
[23] Cf. ibid., no. 30.
[24] *Lumen Gentium*, 25.
[25] Ibid.
[26] Vatican II, *Gaudium et Spes*, 16.
[27] Cf. CCC 1777.
[28] Vatican II, *Dignitatis Humanae*, 16.

principles given by God and taught by the Church are for our own good. Because of original sin, we are very vulnerable to sexual temptations and disorders. With God's grace, however, we can grow in holiness, wisdom, and chastity.

CHAPTER ELEVEN

GROWING IN CHASTITY

The Catholic understanding of human sexuality has four main characteristics: (1) It is realistic; (2) it is challenging; (3) it is compassionate; and (4) it is true.

The *realism* of Catholic sexual morality is rooted in a sound anthropology that recognizes the weakness of the flesh and the grandeur of human dignity. Behind this realism is the awareness of the power of *eros* and its need for purification. As Pope Benedict XVI writes: "True, *eros* tends to rise 'in ecstasy' to the Divine, to lead us beyond ourselves; yet for this very reason it calls for a path of ascent, renunciation, purification, and healing."[1]

Without purification and healing, sexual desire can become a chaotic, self-serving, and destructive energy. The Church recognizes that *eros* is rooted in man's very nature and, as such, "directs man toward marriage, to a bond which is unique and definitive" because it corresponds to the "exclusive and definitive love" between the one God and his people.[2]

Along with the Church's realism comes the challenge of chastity. To live according to Catholic moral teaching is *challenging* because it requires self-control, prayer, and vigilance. Part of this challenge comes from a culture that extols sexual self-indulgence rather than authentic love. Living chastely is especially challenging for those who are single, widowed, or divorced. Loneliness, hurt, and depression can make single people very prone to sexual

---

[1] Benedict XVI, *Deus Caritas Est*, 5.
[2] Ibid., no. 11.

temptations and abuse. The alluring but destructive traps of pornography, masturbation, fornication, and manipulative relations can be very real. Along with prayer, there is the need to develop chaste friendships, where people are appreciated for their ideas and interests rather than how they relate to sexual needs.

Catholic sexual morality is rooted in *compassion*. The Church understands how easy it is to fall into sexual sins out of human weakness and loneliness. The sacrament of confession is a great gift for those who are struggling with chastity. Failures due to human weakness should be brought to Christ, the Good Shepherd, who expresses his mercy and forgiveness through the ministry of the priest. Those guilty of sexual sins are blessed when they recognize their need for divine forgiveness. Those who justify their sexual sins are the ones in serious danger because they rationalize their wrongdoing. In the Gospels, Jesus shows great love for those who have fallen into sexual sins (cf. Jn 4:16–26; Jn 8:10–11). He is ready to offer the same love and mercy today to those who commit such sins.

Finally, Catholic sexual morality is *true*. It has stood the test of time because it is rooted in the truth revealed to us by God. The failure to recognize the true meaning and purpose of human sexuality has left its sad, desperate mark on human history. How many broken hearts and homes have there been because of the abuse of this great gift!

Practical Advice for Chastity in the Different States of Life

Chastity, as we have seen, is "the successful integration of sexuality within the person"[3] and a "fruit of the Holy Spirit."[4] As such, chastity requires both human discipline and supernatural assistance. Chastity also is lived out differently according to the different states of life. In what follows, some suggestions for growing in

---

[3] CCC 2337.
[4] Cf. ibid., 1832, and Gal 5:22–23.

chastity (by no means exhaustive) are given for the different states of life:

1. Single People

Those who are single and open to marriage should develop chaste friendships with those of the opposite sex, and they must learn that not every friendship need be entered into as a prelude to marriage. The emphasis on friendship rather than "going out" or "dating" can help ease tension and remove the tendency to envision every friend of the opposite sex as a possible future spouse; and often it is advisable to go out in groups. When friendships develop into deeper affection and attraction, then steps should be taken to avoid inappropriate displays of physical affection that can lead to violations of chastity.

Some single people find it difficult to form friendships with those of the opposite sex, or they feel inadequate and awkward. Failures to form good friendships with those of the opposite sex can lead to temptations of fantasy, pornography, and masturbation (and sometimes homosexuality). Such temptations, when not resisted, can further hinder a person's ability to form chaste friendships. Either a person will become isolated and live in a fantasy world or the person will seek relations focused on sexual activity rather than true communication and affection.

Single people open to marriage should understand that the cultivation of chastity *before* marriage helps prepare them for the challenges of chastity *in* marriage. This is why it is so important to seek friendships with members of the opposite sex who are committed to the same moral and religious standards. They should also look for qualities of a good future father or mother. If the friendship becomes more intimate, a strong moral and religious commitment is needed on the part of *both* people to keep the relationship chaste.

Some single people might be open to marriage, but they never marry because the right person does not enter their lives. A strong spiritual life is needed for such single people because loneliness or broken relations can lead them to temptations such as fantasy, masturbation, and pornography. On the human level, such single people should cultivate wholesome and chaste activities such as sports, reading, or travel. Volunteer work, especially with the poor, helps people prone to loneliness to move beyond their own needs and potential temptations. People who are single and have yet to find a spouse might also ask whether God is calling them to religious life or the priesthood. This, of course, is not always the case. Some people are called by God to live as single people who contribute their own special gifts to the Body of Christ.

2. Married People

Many aspects of marital chastity have already been treated. There are, however, a few points that can be added. Married people need to cultivate chastity in harmony with the love they have for their spouses. In other words, a married man or woman must treat sexual matters within the context of spousal love. This means that husbands and wives must never look upon anyone other than their spouses as objects of sexual desire. The total and exclusive nature of spousal love prohibits this. For married people, such feelings of lust are offenses against the love they should have for their spouses.

Married men are especially prone to such temptations. Often, married men believe there is nothing wrong with admiring the physical beauty of women other than their wives. Such glances of admiration, however, can easily become lustful. When married men indulge in pornography or sexual fantasies, they are not only violating objective standards of sexual morality; they are also failing in their love for their spouses.

Unfortunately, our culture tends to place too much importance on physical beauty and youth. Some men expect their wives to look the same at 40 or 50 as they did when they were 25 (often without placing similar expectations on themselves!). The love they have for their wives should involve more than attraction to youth and physical beauty. True love must deepen with age and be sustained by spousal communication and friendship. Marital chastity must develop within a context of prayer and shared spiritual values.

Married men and women who have professional contacts with those of the opposite sex might sometimes feel strong attractions to women and men other than their spouses. Such attractions can emerge spontaneously and unexpectedly.[5] In such cases, there is a need to maintain proper, professional limits — especially if the attraction seems mutual. If friendships develop, it will always be important not to say or do anything that could suggest a personal interest beyond what is appropriate. The old advice of avoiding the "near occasions of sin" seems warranted, and married men and women should remind themselves of their love and commitment to their spouses before allowing any such attractions to move beyond a purity of heart.[6]

3. The Widowed and the Divorced

Those who are widowed and divorced have their own unique challenges with regard to chastity. Without the support of prayer and friendship, those who find themselves single after many years of marriage can be easily prone to the sexual temptations connected with loneliness. Those who are widowed often find support from their children and the memories of their deceased spouse. Some who are widowed sometimes seek friendships with those of the opposite sex and are open to remarriage. Others who are widowed gradually settle into the single life and develop interests that sustain them.

Those who are divorced, especially the young, have special challenges with chastity. Sometimes there is a fear of entering into another committed relationship, so there is a complete renunciation of any relations with the opposite sex. Other divorced people

---

[5] Needless to say, it is not sinful for married persons to notice the physical attractiveness of women and men other than their spouses. Nor is it sinful for them to find some personalities attractive and interesting. It would be sinful, however, for them to entertain lustful or covetous thoughts about women and men who are not their spouses.

[6] Cf. CCC 2517–2533 with regard to the "purification of the heart" required by the ninth commandment: "You shall not covet your neighbor's wife."

immediately begin looking for a replacement and sometimes enter into sexual relationships lacking the commitment of marriage.

Divorced Catholics should explore the possibility of a declaration of nullity (annulment) if they believe they might wish to marry again. Sometimes the process involves too much pain, so it is never pursued beyond the initial steps. Parishes usually provide special pastoral services to those who are divorced to help assist them if they wish to seek an annulment.[7] Unless an annulment is received, a divorced Catholic is not free to marry in the Catholic Church.

Sometimes, divorced Catholics have no desire to marry again. If this is the case, then they are called to live chastely as single people (though, of course, the marriage bond remains unless the Church has recognized its nullity). To live as a chaste single person might require some adjustment, but, with God's grace, it can be done. The support of prayer, friendships, and the sacraments can help divorced people live happy lives separated from their spouses.

4. Those Living in Chaste Celibacy as Priests and Consecrated Religious

The recent sex scandals involving Catholic clergy show that celibate priests and religious are prone to the most deviant form of sexual behavior, the abuse of minors. Other lapses from chastity on the parts of priests and religious are also disturbing, even when there are two consenting adults involved. The sexual sins of priests and religious are truly scandalous because the faithful look upon these men and women with deep respect and admiration and hold them to a higher standard. In his 1954 encyclical, *Sacra Virginitas*, Pope Pius XII noted that those who have consecrated themselves to live as virgins receive from God a spiritual gift that "immeasurably surpasses" the mutual assistance given to spouses in marriage.[8] In other words, those who consecrate themselves to the Lord as

---

[7] There are other support groups available as well, such as The Ministry of the North American Conference of Separated and Divorced Catholics (http://www.nacsdc.org).

[8] Pius XII, *Sacra Virginitas*; Denz.-H, 3912.

chaste celibates receive the spiritual support proportionate to the high calling of their state.

It is sometimes said that there is nothing worse than a monk or a nun who does not pray. The same can be said for celibate priests who neglect the Liturgy of the Hours and the faithful celebration of the Eucharist. It is only by fidelity to the life of prayer that those in the celibate state of life can live chastely.

The celibate life does involve the renunciation of the good of marriage, but it does not involve a renunciation of being a man or a woman. As Pope John Paul II has eloquently taught, consecrated celibacy is not simply a renunciation but also an affirmation; it is an affirmation of "the spousal meaning of body" in which there is a "sincere gift of self" to Christ.[9] Chaste celibacy is an expression of "*the dignity of the personal gift* connected with the spousal meaning of the body in its masculinity and femininity."[10]

The Church believes consecrated celibacy is a precious gift to the Body of Christ. Those who have consecrated themselves to the Lord in virginity and chaste celibacy provide a "sign that can and ought to attract all the members of the Church to an effective and prompt fulfillment of their Christian vocation."[11] Those who embrace the three evangelical counsels manifest to all believers "the presence of the heavenly goods already possessed here below," and they point us "to the future resurrection and the glory of the heavenly kingdom."[12] Some of the most joyful people I have ever met have been chaste celibates. Men and women who embody serene and joyful celibacy provide a great witness to the Church, a witness that has proven to be spiritually fruitful in every age.

All of the faithful, whatever their state in life, should rely upon the intercession of the Blessed Virgin Mary, St. Joseph, the angels, and the saints. For priests and religious, the intercession of Mary is especially important. Mary, the Mother of the Incarnate Word,

---

[9] John Paul II, General Audience, May 5, 1982; *Man and Woman*, 442.
[10] Ibid., 443 (emphasis in original).
[11] *Lumen Gentium*, 44.
[12] Ibid.

"stands out in eminent and singular fashion as an exemplar of both virgin and mother."[13] As the virgin spouse of the Holy Spirit, Mary shines forth as the supreme model of human love, elevated and glorified, serving as our "model of virtues"[14] and "our Mother in the order of grace."[15]

Final Thoughts

God created us as sexual beings, male and female. We cannot pretend that we are asexual beings like the angels. We should accept our masculinity or femininity as a gift given to us by God. Because of original sin, however, the great gift of human sexuality has been subject to incredible distortion and abuse. The Catholic Church is fully conscious of the power of human sexual desire and the hazards of *eros* not purified and elevated by self-sacrificing love. In this book, I have tried to present Catholic sexual morality in a positive yet realistic light. The harms caused by sexual immorality are visible to all with open eyes: broken marriages, abortions, exploited women, lonely hearts, and human beings reduced to objects of pleasure.

Many people still consider Catholic sexual morality to be outdated, a thing of the past. I wonder, though, whether the new sexual morality is really contributing to true happiness, better marriages, and deeper love. I hope people will take a second look at the traditional teachings of the Catholic Church on sexual matters. I am convinced that this morality is grounded in the truth of what God wants for us as men and women called to love and bring forth new life. It is a morality that is realistic, challenging, compassionate, and true. May God give us the courage and wisdom to embrace and defend the good news of Catholic sexual morality!

---

[13] Ibid., 63.
[14] Ibid., 65.
[15] Ibid., 61.

THE ESSENTIAL ENDS AND PROPERTIES OF MARRIAGE: IS THERE A HIERARCHY?

What are the essential ends and properties of marriage? St. Augustine, as we have seen, underscored the three goods (*bona*) of marriage: offspring, fidelity, and sacrament. Building on these basic goods of marriage, Catholic tradition, since the late nineteenth century, has also spoken more specifically of the "ends" and "essential properties" of marriage.

In his 1880 encyclical, *Arcarnum Divinae Sapientiae*, Pope Leo XIII points to "unity and indissolubility" as the "two most excellent properties" of marriage.[1] In the same encyclical, he sees the purposes of marriage (procreation, mutual help, faithful love, and sacrament) as all interconnected:

> Not only, in strict truth, was marriage instituted for the propagation of the human race, but also that the lives of husbands and wives might be made better and happier. This comes about in many ways: by their lightening each other's burdens through mutual help; by constant and faithful love; by having all their possessions in common; and by the heavenly grace that flows from the Sacrament.[2]

---

[1] Leo XIII, Encyclical, *Arcanum Divinae Sapientiae*, 5, in *Marriage: Papal Teachings*, selected by the Benedictine Monks of Solesmes, trans. Michael J. Byrnes (Boston: Daughters of St. Paul, 1963), no. 148, p. 135.

[2] Leo XIII, *Arcanum*, 26, in *Marriage: Papal Teachings*, no. 174, p. 152.

Do any of these ends of marriage have priority? Leo XIII does not provide a "ranking" of these ends in *Arcanum*. But in his 1891 encyclical, *Rerum Novarum*, in defending the rights of the family from state control, he points to procreation as "the chief and principal purpose of marriage." As he writes:

> No human law can abolish the natural and original right of marriage, nor in any way limit the chief and principal purpose of marriage ordained by God's authority from the beginning: "Increase and multiply."[3]

This recognition of procreation as the primary end (*finis primarius*) of marriage became standard in the Catholic theology of the late nineteenth and early twentieth centuries. It made its way into the 1917 *Code of Canon Law*, which provided a succinct summary of the ends and essential features of the sacrament of matrimony:

> Canon 1013. # 1. The primary end of marriage is the procreation and education of children; the secondary ends are mutual help and the remedy of concupiscence (*Matrimonii finis primarius est procreatio atque educatio prolis; secundarius mutuum adiutorium et remedium concupiscentiae*).

> # 2. The essential properties of marriage are unity and indissolubility, which obtain a special solidity in Christian marriage by reason of the sacrament (*Essentiales matrimonii proprietates sunt unitas ac indissolubilitas, quae in matrimonio christiano peculiarem obtinent firmitatem ratione sacramenti*).[4]

Pius XI refers specifically to Canon 1013.1 of the 1917 *Code* in his 1930 encyclical, *Casti Conubii*,[5] but he also makes it clear that sexual intercourse within marriage can be justified for reasons other than procreation if the latter is not possible:

---

[3] Leo XIII, *Rerum Novarum*, 12, in *Marriage: Papal Teachings*, no. 210, pp. 173–174.

[4] *Codex Iuris Canonici Pii X Pontificis Maximi Iussa Digestus Benedicti Papae XV Auctoritate Promulgatus* (Westminster, MD: The Newman Press, 1964). Canon 1013, p. 341.

[5] Pius XI, *Casti Connubii*, 17, in *Matrimony: Papal Teachings*, no. 279, p. 228.

Nor are husband and wife to be accused of acting against nature if they make use of their right in a proper and natural manner, even though natural causes (due to circumstances of time or to certain defects) render it impossible for new life to originate. Both matrimony and the use of the matrimonial right (*in coniugalis iuris usu*) have secondary ends — such as mutual help (*mutuum adiutorium*), the fostering of reciprocal love (*mutuusque fovendus amor*), and the abasement of concupiscence (*concupiscentiae sedatio*) — which husband and wife are quite entitled to have in view, so long as the intrinsic nature of the act, and therefore its due subordination to its primary end, is safeguarded.[6]

In this passage, we see that Pius XI has added the "fostering of reciprocal love" to the list of valid secondary ends of the marital act, even though it was not mentioned in Canon 1013.1 of the 1917 *Code*.

During the pontificate of Pius XII (in 1944), the question was put before the Holy Office: "Whether the opinion of certain recent [authors] could be admitted who either deny that the primary end of marriage is the generation and education of children or who teach that the secondary ends are not essentially subordinate to the primary end, but are equally primary and independent?"[7] The response (which was confirmed by the Pope) was "No."

This response was in line with the 1917 *Code of Canon Law*, but it did not preclude further theological development. Pius XII, in his 1951 "Allocution to the Midwives," upholds "procreation and upbringing of new life" as the primary end of marriage — "as an institution of nature" (*come istituzione naturale*).[8] He makes it clear, however, that this primary end of marriage should not lead to a "denying or diminishing what is good and just in personal values

---

[6] Ibid., no. 319 (p. 250).

[7] Denz.-H, 3838.

[8] Pius XII, "Allocution to the Midwives," Oct. 29, 1951, in *Matrimony: Papal Teachings*, no. 633, p. 424.

resulting from matrimony and its realization."[9] Pius XII goes on to say that "the conjugal act, ordained and desired by nature, is a personal cooperation, to which husband and wife, when contracting marriage, exchange the right."[10] He then feels compelled to defend "the human dignity" of the conjugal act in these words:

> The same Creator, Who in His bounty and wisdom willed to make use of the work of man and woman, by uniting them in matrimony, for the preservation and propagation of the human race, has also decreed that in this function the parties should experience pleasure and happiness of body and spirit. Husband and wife, therefore, by seeking and enjoying this pleasure, do no wrong whatever. They accept what the Creator has destined for them.[11]

Pius XII goes on, however, to warn couples not to "abandon themselves without restraint to the impulses of the senses."[12] He then offers this succinct summary of the Catholic teaching:

> The right rule is this: the use of the natural procreative disposition is morally lawful in matrimony only, in the service of and in accordance with the ends of marriage itself. Hence it follows that only in marriage with the observing of this rule is the desire and the fruition of this pleasure and of this satisfaction lawful. For the pleasure is subordinate to the law of action whence it derives, and not vice versa — the action to the law of pleasure.[13]

In addition to his recognition of "the pleasure and happiness of body and spirit" derived from sexual union, Pius also points to the personal and spiritual dimensions of conjugal love (*amore coniugale*).[14] He makes it clear that the conjugal act within marriage cannot be reduced "to a mere organic function for the transmission of

---

[9] Ibid., no. 635, p. 426.
[10] Ibid., no. 638, p. 428.
[11] Ibid., no. 643, p. 430.
[12] Ibid., no. 644, p. 430.
[13] Ibid., no. 644, pp. 430–431.
[14] Ibid., no. 636, p. 427.

seed."[15] Anticipating to some extent "the theology of the body," Pius XII speaks of the conjugal act as "a personal action," which, by its very structure, "is the expression of the reciprocal gift, which, according to Holy Writ, effects the union 'in one flesh.'"[16] This marital union, however, can never be separated from "the service of life," because conjugal love is "subordinated and ordered to the great law of the '*generatio et educatio prolis*' (the generation and education of children), namely the accomplishment of the primary end of matrimony as the origin and source of life."[17]

From these insights of Pius XII, we can see the basic framework of the doctrine of marital love found in Vatican II's *Pastoral Constitution on the Church in the Modern World* (*Gaudium et Spes*). The beauty and dignity of conjugal love is highlighted,[18] but there is also the recognition that this love is ordered to the procreation and education of children. Two passages from *Gaudium et Spes* bring out this point:

> By its very nature the institution of marriage and married love is ordered to the procreation and education of children and it is in them that it finds its crowning glory. (GS, 48)

> Marriage and married love (*amor coniugalis*) are by nature ordered (*ordinantur*) to the procreation and education of children. Indeed, children are the supreme gift of marriage and greatly contribute to the good of the parents themselves. (GS, 50)

These passages are certainly in harmony with the procreation and education of children as the "primary end" of marriage. Indeed, children supply the marriage with its "crowning glory" (*suo fastigio coronantur*) and are its "supreme gift" (*praestantissimum donum*). The Council Fathers, however, chose not use the language of the primary and secondary ends of marriage as found in the 1917 *Code of Canon Law*. Instead, there was an effort to show how "the intimate

---

15 Ibid., no. 637, p. 427.
16 Ibid.
17 Ibid., no. 646, p. 432.
18 See especially *Gaudium et Spes*, 49.

partnership of life and love which constitutes the married state" serves "the good of the partners, of the children, and of society."[19]

This ordering of the marital covenant toward both the good of the spouses and the good of the children makes its way into the 1983 *Code of Canon Law*. In Canon 1055.1, this description of marriage is given:

> The matrimonial covenant, by which a man and a woman establish between themselves a partnership of the whole of life and which is ordered by its nature to the good of the spouses and the procreation and education of offspring, has been raised by Christ the Lord to the dignity of a sacrament between the baptized.[20]

This description of marriage is found in the *Catechism of the Catholic Church*, 1601, which refers to both Canon 1055.1 and *Gaudium et Spes* 48. Since the 1983 *Code of Canon Law* no longer speaks of the primary and secondary ends of marriage, some have claimed that a new concept of marriage is now operative.[21] This, though, seems difficult to sustain because *Canon* 1056 of the 1983 Code repeats what Canon 1013.2 of the 1917 *Code* describes as the essential properties of marriage, namely "unity and indissolubility." Why, though, was the prior language of the primary and secondary ends omitted? Three explanations seem possible.

First, it can be argued that Vatican II does not actually deny the primacy of the procreation and education of children as a natural end of marriage.[22] The council fathers, however, wished to underscore the intimate connection between the good of the spouses and the good of the children. After all, procreation is pursued through the

---

[19] *Gaudium et Spes*, 48. For a canonical discussion of "the good of the spouses" (*bonum coniugum*) see Cormac Burke, "The *Bonum Coniugum* and the *Bonum Prolis*: Ends or Properties of Marriage?" *The Jurist* 49 (1989), 704–713.

[20] The translation is taken from the Vatican Web site.

[21] For a "tradionalist" Catholic perspective, see Rev. Peter R. Scott, "Questions and Answers," *The Angelus*, vol. XXIV, no. 10 (October 1989). This article can be found online at http://www.sspx.ca/Angelus_October/Questions_Answers.htm.

[22] On this point, see Waldstein, 693 [Index] where references are made to passages from John Paul II that still affirm procreation as "the essential end of marriage." See also Karol Wojtyla, *Love and Responsibility*, trans. H.T. Willetts (San Francisco, Ignatius Press, 1993), 68. Procreation is spoken of as the primary end of marriage, but it is an end that is never separate from love.

conjugal union of the spouses, and the essential properties of marriage — unity and indissolubility — serve the good of both the spouses and children. *Gaudium et Spes* 48 highlights this reality:

> Thus the man and woman, who "are no longer two but one" (Mt 19:6), help and serve each other by their marriage partnership; they become conscious of their unity and experience it more deeply from day to day. The intimate union of marriage, as a mutual giving of two persons, and the good of the children demand total fidelity from the spouses and require an unbreakable unity between them.

Gaudium et Spes 50 also notes how children, "as the supreme gift of marriage, ... greatly contribute to the good of the parents themselves." Thus, the good of the parents is served by their cooperation with God's command to "be fruitful and multiply" (Gen 1:28). *Gaudium et Spes* 50 continues with another affirmation of the procreative ordering of married life:

> Without intending to underestimate the other ends of marriage, it must be said that true married love and the whole structure of family life which results from it is directed to disposing the spouses to cooperate valiantly with the love of the Creator and the Savior, who through them will increase and enrich his family from day to day.

Since the 1983 *Code of Canon Law* draws upon the teaching of Vatican II (and prior councils), it seems that the ordering of the whole structure of married life toward procreation is still very much part of Catholic teaching. The ordering of marriage toward procreation, however, can never be divorced from the mutual love and support of the spouses.[23] Therefore, listing these ends as primary and secondary could lead to misunderstanding.

---

[23] On this point, see Dietrich von Hildebrand, *The Encyclical Humanae Vitae: A Sign of Contradiction* (Chicago: Franciscan Herald Press, 1969), 34–35: "The God-given essential link between love of man and woman and its fulfillment in the marital union, on the one hand, and the creation of a new person, on the other hand, has precisely the character of superabundance, which is a much deeper connection than would be one of merely instrumental finality."

From this follows a *second reason* why Vatican II and the 1983 *Code* do not explicitly refer to the primary and secondary ends of marriage. The "good of the spouses" is so essential to marriage *as a sacrament* that describing it as a "secondary end" might obscure its significance. Furthermore, when procreation is spoken of as the primary end of marriage, it could suggest that marriages that fail to produce children (through no fault of the spouses) are marriages that have fallen short of the principal end of the sacrament. Such marriages might erroneously be looked upon as flawed — even if the spouses very much wanted children of their own.

We must remember that the sacraments are directed to human sanctification;[24] so a major purpose of the sacrament of matrimony is to foster the sanctification of the spouses. This sanctification represents the "good of the spouses" in a preeminent way. Clearly, the procreation and education of children contributes immensely to this sanctification, but God instituted marriage for the good of both the spouses and the children. This is expressed in Gen. 2:18–24, where the unitive meaning of conjugal union is revealed, and in Gen. 1:28, where the procreative meaning is manifested. Paul Pope VI, as we have seen, speaks of an "unbreakable connection" (*nexu indissolubili*) between the unitive meaning and the procreative meaning [of the conjugal act].[25]

The "universal call to holiness" is one of the major themes of Vatican II.[26] The Council explains how the sacrament of marriage contributes to this call to holiness:

> Finally, in virtue of the sacrament of Matrimony by which [the faithful] signify and share (cf. Eph 5:32) the mystery of the unity and faithful love between Christ and the Church, Christian married couples help one another to attain holiness in their married life and in the rearing of their children.[27]

---

[24] Cf. CCC 1123.

[25] Paul VI, *Humanae Vitae*, 12; trans. Janet E. Smith, *Humanae Vitae: A Generation Later*, 281.

[26] See especially, *Lumen Gentium*, 39–42.

[27] *Lumen Gentium*, 11

Christian married couples and parents, following their own way, should support one another in grace all through life with faithful love, and should train their children (lovingly received from God) in Christian doctrine and evangelical virtues.[28]

From this, we see that the description of marriage given in the 1983 *Code* and the *Catechism of the Catholic Church* incorporates what Vatican II teaches about marriage: it is a way of holiness for both the spouses and their children. As a sacramental covenant, marriage "is by its nature ordered toward the good of the spouses and the procreation and education of children."[29] The "good of the spouses," however, goes beyond a merely natural perfection in virtue; it is ultimately oriented to the life of grace and blessedness.

As a general concept, "the good of the spouses" — though apparently new as a canonical term[30] — is hardly foreign to the Catholic tradition. In an article originally published in 1961,[31] Fr. Paul Quay finds in Aquinas a distinction between the *essential* ends of marriage (of which procreation has priority) and the more *excellent* ends of marriage (of which "sacrament" has priority). Aquinas responds to the question, "Whether the sacrament is the chief of the marriage goods?" He notes that the three goods of marriage (offspring, faith, and sacrament) can be considered in terms of what is more essential or more excellent. In terms of what is more excellent, he writes that "'sacrament' is in every way the most important of the three marriage goods, since it belongs to marriage considered as a sacrament of grace, while the other two belong to it as an office of nature."[32]

---

[28] Ibid., 41.

[29] CCC 1601.

[30] Cf. article by Cormac Burke in *The Jurist* cited in note 19.

[31] Paul M. Quay, S.J., "Contraception and Conjugal Love," *Theological Studies* 22 (1961): 18–40; republished in *Why Humanae Vitae Was Right: A Reader*, Janet E. Smith, ed. (San Francisco: Ignatius Press, 1993), 17–46.

[32] Aquinas, *Summa theologicae*, trans. Fathers of the English Dominican Province [1920] (Allen, TX: Christian Classics [reprint], 1981) supplement, q. 49, a. 3. All subsequent translations from the *Summa theologicae* are taken from this edition, which is also posted online at http://www.newadvent.org/summa/504903.htm. It should be noted that Fr. Quay speaks of the "ends" of marriage, whereas Aquinas here speaks off the "goods" of marriage.

In a similar way, Aquinas observes that the good of offspring could be honored with a plurality of wives but not the good of sacrament.[33] To be sure, St. Thomas believes that the intentions to have offspring and fidelity are essential to the marriage pact itself, so that if anything contrary to these were expressed in the marital consent, "the marriage would be invalid."[34] Nevertheless, because the good of "sacrament" belongs to the perfection of grace rather than a perfection of nature, it would have priority in terms of excellence. If the "good of the spouses" is understood in terms of the "perfection of grace" that comes from the sacrament, then we can see why it should not be considered a secondary end of marriage.

These insights of Aquinas explain a *third reason* for not referring to the primary and secondary ends of marriage. Vatican II wished to acknowledge certain aspects of the Catholic tradition on marriage other than those reflected in the 1917 *Code*.[35] In preparing the text of *Gaudium et Spes*, 190 of the council fathers asked that the traditional hierarchy of the marital ends be included.[36] By way of response, it was noted that, in a pastoral document, such juridical precision is not required.[37] Moreover, it was observed that the hierarchy of the goods of marriage could be considered under diverse aspects.[38] References were made to St. Augustine (*De bono coniugii*; PL 40, 375–376 and 394), St. Thomas Aquinas (*Summa Theol., Suppl.* Q. 49, art. 3, ad 1), the Council of Florence (*Decree for the Armenians*, Denz.-H., 1327), and Pius XI (*Casti Connubii*: AAS 22 [1930], 547–548). These texts show that

---

[33] Aquinas, *Summa Theologicae*, supplement, q. 65, a. 1.

[34] Ibid., q. 49, a. 3.

[35] Needless to say, what is taught in the 1917 *Code* reflects an important theological insight. The Magisterium, however, never proposed this teaching in a definitive manner that precluded subsequent development. The key insight of the 1917 Code on procreation as a primary natural end of marriage has been retained, even if it is now placed in a larger context.

[36] Cf. *Acta Synodalia Sacrosancti Concilii Vaticani II*, vol. 4, pars VII, (Rome: Typis Polyglottis Vaticanis, 1978), 477; see also Janet E. Smith, *Humanae Vitae: A Generation Later*, 48.

[37] Ibid.

[38] *Acta Synodalia*, vol. 4, pars VII, 478.

the purposes of marriage can be considered not only according to "the order of nature" but also with respect to the "Christian goods" of the sacrament.[39] In fact, Pius XI (in the cited text of *Casti Connubii*) actually refers to the perfection of the spouses as "the primary cause and reason of marriage." As he writes:

> This mutual interior formation of husband and wife, this persevering endeavor to bring each other to the state of perfection, may in a true sense be called, as the *Roman Catechism* calls it, the primary cause and reason of matrimony (*primaria matrimonii causa et ratio*), so long as marriage is considered not in its stricter sense, as the institution destined for the procreation and education of children, but in the wider sense as a complete and intimate life-partnership and association (*totius vitae communio, consuetudo, societas*)[40]

The passage of the *Roman Catechism* referenced by Pius XI indicates that the first reason (*prima ... ratio*) for marriage is that "nature itself by an instinct implanted in both sexes impels them to such companionship, and this is further encouraged by the hope of mutual assistance, in bearing more easily the discomforts of life and the infirmities of old age."[41] The "desire for a family" is given as the second reason for marriage.[42] Here we see that the *Roman Catechism* understands the desire for companionship and mutual assistance as the primary reason for marriage, while the 1917 *Code of Canon Law* lists "mutual help" as a secondary end of marriage. A distinction, of course, could be made between the "reasons" and the "ends" of marriage, but this only shows how the language of primary and secondary purposes can be open to misunderstanding.

Pius XI's reference to marriage as an "intimate life-partnership and association" is reflected in Canon 1055 of the 1983 *Code*,

---

[39] Ibid., 477. These same texts are also cited in a footnote to *Gaudium et Spes*, 48.
[40] Pius XI, *Casti Connubii*, 24, in *Matrimony: Papal Teachings*, no. 287, pp. 231–232; cf. AAS 22 (1930), 548–549. See also *Catech. Rom.*, part II, chap. VIII, q. 13 (cited by Pius XI).
[41] *The Catechism of the Council of Trent*, trans. McHugh and Callan, 343–344.
[42] Ibid., 344.

which refers to marriage as a "partnership for the whole of life" (*totius vitae consortium*). It appears that this passage of *Casti Connubii* was an important source for both *Gaudium et Spes* and the 1983 *Code*.[43]

It must be emphasized, however, that both *Gaudium et Spes* and the 1983 *Code* clearly teach that the matrimonial covenant "is by nature ordered toward the good of the spouses *and* the procreation and education of offspring."[44] Procreation remains fundamental to the natural ordering of marriage, and spouses who refuse to pursue this end are acting against the natural and divine purpose of the sacrament. Moreover, there is a certain truth to what was taught by the Holy Office in 1944: the other ends of marriage can never be understood as independent of the duty of the spouses toward their offspring.[45] The good of the spouses is always intimately linked to the procreation and education of children.[46]

---

[43] The influence of *Casti Connubii* on the 1983 *Code* is noted by William E. May in his article, "Love Between Man and Woman: The Epitome of Love," which was originally published in Italian as "L'amore fra uomo e donna: archetipo di amore per excellenza," in *La via dell'amore: Riflessioni sull'enciclica "Deus caritas est: di Benedetto XVI*," edited by Livio Melina and Carl Anderson (Rome: Pontificio Instituto Giovanni Paolo II per Studi su matrimonio e famiglia, 2006) pp. 47–58. An English version of this article can be found on Professor's May's home page at the John Paul II Institute in Washington, D.C. and online at http://www.christendom-awake.org/pages/may/lovebetween.htm.

[44] *Codex Iuris Canonici* [1983], canon 1055.1 (emphasis added).

[45] Cf. Denz.-H.

[46] As was noted earlier, this does not mean spouses who, through no fault of their own, fail to have children are in a flawed marriage. For spouses blessed with children, however, there is a certain subordination of their own desires and needs to the good of their children and, likewise, a natural ordination of the sexual act to the good of procreation. In 1944, the Holy Office wished to uphold these values by means of its ruling.

GUIDANCE FROM THE CHURCH: A SUMMARY OF KEY MAGISTERIAL DOCUMENTS

Leo XIII, Encyclical, *Arcanum Divinae Sapientiae* [Feb. 10, 1880]: a beautiful summary of the Catholic understanding of the sacrament of marriage, and also a defense of the Church's rightful authority with respect to this sacrament. (http://www.vatican.va/holy_father/leo_xiii/encyclicals/documents/hf_1-xii_enc_10021880_arcanum_en.html)

Pope Pius XI, Encyclical, *Casti Connubii* [Dec. 31, 1930]: following the Anglican Lambeth Conference of 1930 (which permitted the use of contraceptives by married couples for serious reasons), Pius XI reaffirms the Catholic understanding of the "sacred partnership" of marriage grounded in the three "goods" of offspring, fidelity, and sacrament. The encyclical also condemns various offenses to marriage, including divorce, adultery, sterilization, and contraception. Although Pius XI allows couples to have recourse to intercourse during infertile times, he speaks of contraceptive acts as contrary to the law of God and nature. He strongly condemns abortion, and he urges Catholics to choose marriage partners giving first place "to the consideration of God and the true religion of Christ."(http://www.vatican.va/holy_father/pius_xi/encyclicals/documents/hf_p-xi_enc_31121930_casti-connubii_en.html)

Pius XII, *Allocution to the Midwives* [Oct. 29, 1951]: the Holy Father affirms the dignity of the marital act as well as the happiness and pleasure, willed by the Creator, that the spouses experience. He warns, however, about the dangers of hedonism, and he points out that, as an institution of nature, marriage is ordered primarily to the procreation and education of children. Married couples, for serious motives and grave reasons, may limit conjugal relations to "the natural sterile periods." Direct acts of contraception, however, are "intrinsically immoral," and direct sterilization is "a grave violation of the moral law." (http://ewtn.com/library/PAPALDOC/P511029.HTM)

Pius XII, Encyclical, *Sacra Virginitas* [Mar. 25, 1954]: the Holy Father responds to those who claim that, because marriage is a sacrament, it is a more efficacious means than consecrated virginity for achieving union with God. He points out that the life of perfect chastity is not at all a diminishment of the human personality. Instead, it is a state endowed with spiritual gifts that surpass even those of marriage. (http://www.vatican.va/holy_father/pius_xii/encyclicals/documents/hf_p-xii_enc_25031954_sacra-virginitas_en.html)

Vatican II, *Gaudium et Spes* [Dec. 7, 1965]: entitled the *Pastoral Constitution on the Church in the Modern World*, this document provides a rich overview of the Church's understanding of the dignity of marriage and the family (in numbers 47–52). Among the key topics covered are: marriage and the family in today's world (no. 47); the holiness of marriage and the family (no. 48); conjugal love (no. 49); the fruitfulness of marriage (no. 50); harmonizing conjugal love with respect for human life (no. 51); and promoting marriage and the family as the concern of all (no. 52). (http://www.vatican.va/archive/hist_councils/ii_vatican_council/documents/vat-ii_cons_19651207_gaudium-et-spes_en.html)

Paul VI, Encyclical, *Humanae Vitae* [July 25,1968]: during a time when many people were advocating for Church approval of contraception, this encyclical reaffirms the Catholic moral teaching that "each and every marital act must of necessity remained ordered *per se* to the procreation of human life" (no. 11). Paul VI offers a beautiful summary of the four main characteristics of conjugal love as human, total, faithful and exclusive, and fruitful (no. 9). He also highlights the "unbreakable connection" between the unitive and procreative meanings of the conjugal act (no. 12). The Pontiff acknowledges that married couples might decide, for just reasons, to limit sexual intercourse to infertile times in order to avoid pregnancy (no. 14), but, in a prophetic way, he warns of the very serious social consequences that will follow a wider acceptance and practice of contraception (no. 17). (http://www.vatican.va/holy_father/paul_vi /encyclicals/documents/hf_pvi_enc_25071968_humanae-vitae_en. html)

Congregation for the Doctrine of the Faith, *Declaration on Certain Questions concerning Sexual Ethics, Persona Humana* [Dec. 29, 1975]: this document highlights the link between sound sexual ethics and human dignity. It specifically addresses the topics of premarital sex (no. 7); homosexual acts (no. 8); masturbation (no. 9); sexual mortal sins (no. 10); and growth in chastity (no. 11). The document gives sound reasons for upholding traditional Catholic morality on these topics. (http://www.vatican.va/roman_curia/ congregations/cfaith/documents/rc_con_cfaith_doc_19751229_ persona-h...); also available in the volume issued by the Pontifical Council for the Faith, *Enchiridion on the Family* (Boston: Pauline Books & Media, 2004).

John Paul II, Apostolic Exhortation, *The Role of the Christian Family in the Modern World, Familiaris Consortio* [Nov. 22, 1981]: responding to concerns voiced during the Sept. 26–Oct. 25, 1980. synod of bishops in Rome, John Paul II provides a profound and comprehensive overview of the Catholic doctrine on marriage and the family. Highlighting the importance of children as the precious gift of marriage, the Holy Father also presents the family as a "communion of persons" joined together by love. He likewise touches on the rights of women and children, and he condemns the offenses against women's dignity. Underscoring the role of the spouses as cooperators in the love of God, the Creator, John Paul II reaffirms the teaching of *Humanae Vitae* as "the Church's teaching and norm, always old yet always new" (no. 29). (Available online at www.vatican.va and in the *Enchiridion on the Family.*)

John Paul II, Apostolic Constitution, *Sacrae Disciplinae Leges* [Jan. 25, 1983] approving the new Latin *Code of Canon Law*: in canon 1055 of the Code, marriage is described as a "partnership for the whole of life which is ordered by its nature to the good of the spouses and the procreation and education of children." Canon 1056 reaffirms the essential properties of marriage as "unity and indissolubility." (http://www.vatican.va/archive/ENG1104/_P3V.HTM)

The Holy See, *Charter on the Rights of the Family* [Oct. 22, 1983]: this important document contains twelve articles affirming the basic rights of married men and women, families, and children. Among the more important rights are those touching on the freedom from coercion and state control with respect to marriage, procreation, and the education of children. Parents are recognized "as the first and foremost educators of their children" (article 5). The Charter also condemns abortion as "a direct violation of the fundamental right to life of the human being" (article 4). (Found in the *Enchiridion on the Family.*)

Congregation for the Doctrine of the Faith, *Letter to the Bishops of the World on the Pastoral Care of Homosexual Persons* [Oct. 1, 1986]: reacting to some misguided attempts to affirm the legitimacy of homosexual acts, this letter reviews the scriptural and theological reasons why homosexual acts can never be approved. While respecting the dignity of persons with homosexual tendencies, the Congregation makes clear that no pastoral approach can be approved that fails to state clearly that homosexual activity is immoral. (http://www.vatican.va/roman_curia/congregations/cfaith/documents/rc_con_cfaith_doc_19861001_homosexual-persons_en.html)

Congregation for the Doctrine of the Faith, *Instruction on Respect for Human Life in Its Origin and on the Dignity of Procreation, Donum Vitae* [Feb. 22, 1987]: this document affirms the unconditional respect due to human life from the time of conception or fertilization. It condemns research on human embryos that fails to treat them as human persons. Affirming the right of children "to be conceived, carried in the womb and brought into the world, and brought up in marriage" (III A.1), the document speaks out against various forms of artificial reproduction and surrogate motherhood. (Available online at www.vatican.va and in the *Enchiridion on the Family*.)

John Paul II, Apostolic Letter, *Mulieris Dignitatem* [August 15, 1988]: following the Marian Year, this apostolic letter provides a profound biblical and anthropological exploration of the equal dignity of men and women created in the image and likeness of God. It highlights Christ as the great defender of the dignity of women and points to Mary as the model for women as both virgins and mothers.

John Paul II, Apostolic Letter, *Fidei Depositum* [Oct. 11, 1992]: this apostolic letter approves the first edition of the *Catechism of the Catholic Church*, which would be issued in 1997 in its more definitive or "typical" Latin edition. In dealing with the sixth commandment, the *Catechism* provides a fine overview of Catholic moral teaching on chastity and the offenses against chastity (masturbation, fornication, pornography, etc.) in nos. 2347–2400. (The *Catechism* is available online at www.vatican.va.)

John Paul II, Encyclical, *Veritatis Splendor* [Aug. 6, 1993]: this encyclical responds to new forms of moral theology that try to justify immoral acts under certain conditions. The Holy Father reaffirms that there are some actions that are "intrinsically immoral," which can never be approved. Among such intrinsically immoral acts are those of prostitution, adultery, and sexual perversion, which can deprive a person of the kingdom of God (cf. 1 Cor 6:9–10 and nos. 80–81 of the encyclical). (http://www.vatican.va/holy_father/john_paul_ii/encyclicals/documents/hf_jp-ii_enc_06081993_veritatis-splendor_en.html)

John Paul II, *Letter to Families for the International Year of the Family* [Feb. 2, 1994]: welcoming with joy the International Year of the Family declared by the United Nations, the Holy Father provides a beautiful synthesis of the Catholic understanding of the dignity of the family and the beauty and holiness of conjugal love. (Available on vatican.va and in the *Enchiridion on the Family*.)

Congregation for the Doctrine of the Faith, *Letter to the Bishops of the Catholic World concerning the Reception of Holy Communion by Divorced and Remarried Members of the Faithful* [Sept. 124, 1994]: responding to some questionable pastoral practices, this letter reaffirms Catholic teaching that those who are divorced and remarried outside of the Church are in an objective situation that prevents them from worthily receiving Holy Communion (unless a declaration of nullity is granted regarding the prior, putative marriage). (Found in the *Enchiridion on the Family*.)

Pontifical Council for the Family, *The Truth and Meaning of Human Sexuality* [Dec. 8, 1995]: this document provides much valuable material related to training in chastity and the dignity of human sexuality. It also touches on topics such as decency and modesty and reaffirms the role of parents as the primary educators of children (especially in light of some questionable sex education programs). (Found online at www.vatican.va and in the *Enchiridion on the Family*.)

Pontifical Council for the Family, *Preparation for the Sacrament of Marriage* [May 13, 1996]: this document supplies an excellent summary of what is needed for a sound preparation for married life. It covers the remote, proximate, and immediate aspects of preparation. (Found online at www.vatican.va and in the *Enchiridion on the Family*.)

Pontifical Council for the Family, *Vademecum [Guide] for Confessors concerning Some Aspects of the Morality of Conjugal Love* [Feb. 12, 1997]: this document provides a rich overview of the Catholic understanding of marital chastity and responsible parenthood. It underscores the "definitive and irreformable" character of the Church's teaching against contraception (no. 4), and it provides practical guidelines for how confessors should counsel penitents who might be ignorant of the Church's teaching on this matter. (Found online at www.vatican.va and in the *Enchiridion on the Family*.)

John Paul II, Address to the Prelate Auditors, Officials, and Advocates of the Tribunal of the Roman Rota [Jan. 28, 2002]: the Holy Father reaffirms unity and indissolubility as the essential properties of marriage. He urges canon lawyers and tribunal officials to avoid the "divorce mentality" (no. 5). He also instructs civil lawyers to decline using their profession for "an end that is contrary to justice, as is divorce" (no. 9). Lawyers can only cooperate in divorce cases when the intention of the client "is not directed *to the break-up of the marriage* but to *securing of other legitimate effects* that can only be attained through such a judicial process in the established legal order (no. 9; cf. *Catechism of the Catholic Church*, n. 2383; emphasis in original). (Found online at http://www.vatican.va/holy_father/john_paul_ii/ speeches/2002/janurary/documents/hf_jp-ii_spe_20020128_roman-rota_en.html)

Congregation for the Doctrine of the Faith, *Considerations regarding Proposals to Give Legal Recognition to Unions between Homosexual Persons* [June 3, 2003]: this document stresses the obligation of Catholic legislators to uphold the integrity of marriage as a union between one man and one woman. It forbids any kind of support for legal recognition of civil unions between persons of the same sex. (http://www.vatican.va/roman_curia/congregations/cfaith/documents/rc_con_cfaith_doc_20030731_homosexual-unions_en.html)

Congregation for the Doctrine of the Faith, *Letter to the Bishops of the Catholic Church on the Collaboration of Men and Women in the Church and in the World* [May 31, 2004]: this letter eloquently articulates the equal dignity of men and women created in the image and likeness of God. Building upon John Paul II's "theology of the body," it highlights the special and complementary gifts of human beings as male and female. (http://www.vatican.va/roman_curia/congregations/cfaith/documents/rc_con_cfaith_doc_20040731_collaboration_en.html)

Benedict XVI, *Deus Caritas Est* [Dec. 25, 2005]: in his first encyclical, the Holy Father provides a profound reflection on the nature of human and divine love. He examines the different types of love, and he explains how *eros* (love moved by desire) must be purified and directed toward others and toward God in a way expressive of authentic Christian love. (http://www.vatican.va/holy_father/benedict_xvi/encyclicals/documents/hf_ben-xvi_enc_20051225_deus-caritas-est_en.html)

BIBLIOGRAPHY

A few notes: (1) This bibliography does not include works listed in Appendix B, "Guidance from the Church: A Summary of Key Magisterial Documents." (2) Inclusion of a work in this bibliography does not necessarily imply that the author agrees with the contents, opinions, or statements expressed in the work.

Acta Synodalia Sacrosancti Concilii Vaticani II, vol 4, pars VII (Rome: Typis Polyglottis Vaticanis, 1978).

Anatrella, Monsignor Tony. "*Vocation sacerdotale et homosexualité*" *Le portail jeune de l'Église catholique en France* (Oct. 2, 2006: http://www.inxl6.org/article3103.php).

———. "Riflessioni sul documento," *L'Osservatore Romano*, Dec. 15, 2005.

Aquinas, St. Thomas. *Summa Theologica*. Trans. Fathers of the English Dominican Province [1920] (Allen, TX: Christian Classics [reprint], 1981).

Asci, Donald. *The Conjugal Act as a Personal Act* (San Francisco: Ignatius Press, 2002).

Augustine. *The Confessions*. Trans. Rex Warner (New York and Scarborough, Ontario: New American Library, 1963).

Austriaco, Nicanor Pier Giorgio, O.P., "The Myth of the Gay Gene." *Homiletic and Pastoral Review,* vol. CIV, no. 3 (December 2003).

Bonacci, Mary Beth. *Real Love: Mary Beth Bonacci Answers Your Questions on Dating, Marriage and the Real Meaning of Sex* (San Francisco: Ignatius Press, 1996).

Bouscaren, Lincoln T., S.J., and James O'Connor, S.J. *The Canon Law Digest*, vol. 5 (1961), Canon 973 [1917 *Code of Canon Law*], 452–486.

Brouillard, R. "Sanchez, Thomas." In *Dictionnaire de Théologie Catholique*, vol. 14, p. 1 (Paris: Libraire Letouzey et Ané, 1939), 1075–1085.

Burke, Cormac. "The *Bonum Coniugum* and the *Bonum Prolis*: Ends or Properties of Marriage?" *The Jurist* 49 (1989), 704–713.

Cameron, Dr. Paul. *The Gay Nineties: What the Empirical Evidence Reveals about Homosexuality* (Franklin, TN: Adroit Press, 1993).

Catechism of the Catholic Church, Second Edition (Libreria Editrice Vaticana, 1997).

Catechism of the Council of Trent [the *Roman Catechism*]. Trans. John A McHugh, O.P., and Charles J. Callan, O.P. (Rockford, IL: Tan Books and Publishers, 1982).

Catholic League for Religious and Civil Rights. *Sexual Abuse in Social Context: Catholic Clergy and Other Professionals: Special Report by the Catholic League for Religious and Civil Rights* (February 2004: http://www.catholicleague.org/ research/abuse_in_social_context.htm).

Catholic Medical Association. *Homosexuality and Hope* (A.D. 2000). www.cathmed.org.

Cavanaugh, John R., M.D. *Counseling the Homosexual* (Huntington, IN: Our Sunday Visitor, 1977).

Champlin, Fr. Joseph M. "Cohabitation before Marriage." *Catholic Update: June 2003* (Cincinnati, OH: St. Anthony Messenger Press, 2003).

Cline, Dr. Victor. "A Psychologist's View of Pornography." In *The Case against Pornography*, edited by Donald E. Wildmon (Wheaton, IL: Victor Books, 1986), 43–56.

Clowes, Brian W., and David L. Sonnier. "Child Molestation by Homosexuals and Heterosexuals." *Homiletic & Pastoral Review* (May 2005).

Codex Iuris Canonici Pii X Pontificis Maximi Iussa Digestus Benedicti Papae XV Auctoritate Promulgatus (Westminster, MD: The Newman Press, 1964).

Collins, Raymond F. *Divorce in the New Testament* (Collegeville, MN: The Liturgical Press, 1992): 184–213.

Congregation for the Doctrine of the Faith. *The Ecclesial Vocation of the Theologian, Donum Veritatis* (1990) (http://www.vatican.va/roman_curia/congregations/cfaith/documents/rc_con_cfaith_doc_19900524_theologian-vocation_en.html).

Dante. *The Divine Comedy 1: Hell.* Trans. Dorothy Sayers (London: Penguin Books, 1949).

Denzinger, Heinrich, and Peter Hünermann. *Enchiridion symbolorum definitionum et declarationum de rebus fidei et morum.* 40th ed. (Freiburg: Herder, 2005).

Elliot, Peter J. *What God Has Joined: The Sacramentality of Marriage* (New York: Alba House, 1990).

Fagan, Patrick, and Robert E. Rector. "The Effects of Divorce on America" (http://www.heritage.org/research/family/BG1373.cfm).

Fastiggi, Robert. *How to Form Your Catholic Conscience* [pamphlet] (Huntington, IN: Our Sunday Visitor, 2005).

Finn, Bishop Robert W. *Blessed Are the Pure of Heart* (2007) (www.diocese-kcsj.org/Bishop-Finn/pastoral-07.htm).

Flannery Austin, O.P., ed. *Vatican II: The Conciliar and Post Conciliar Documents,* New Revised Edition (Boston, MA: St. Paul Books & Media, 1992).

———. *Vatican II: More Post Conciliar Documents* (Collegeville, MN: The Liturgical Press, 1982).

Ford, John C., S.J., and Gerald Kelly, S.J. *Contemporary Moral Theology, Volume II: Marriage Questions* (Westminster, MD: The Newman Press, 1963).

Ford, John C., S.J., and Germain Grisez. "Contraception and the Infallibility of the Ordinary Magisterium." *Theological Studies* 39:2 (June 1978), 258–312.

Genovesi, Vincent, S.J. *In Pursuit of Love: Catholic Morality and Human Sexuality* (Wilmington, DE: Michael Glazier, Inc., 1987).

Giandurco, Fr. Joseph R., and Fr. John S. Bonnici. *Partners in Life and Love: A Preparation Handbook for the Celebration of Catholic Marriage* (New York: Alba House, 2002).

Grabowski, John S. *Sex and Virtue* (Washington, DC: The Catholic University of America Press, 2003).

Groeschel, Benedict J., OFM Cap. *The Courage to Be Chaste* (New York: Paulist Press, 1985).

Haro, Ramón García de. *Marriage and Family in the Documents of the Magisterium*, Second Edition. Trans. William E. May (San Francisco: Ignatius Press, 1993).

Harvey, John F. "The Pastoral Problem of Masturbation" *Linacre Quarterly*, vol. 60, no. 2 (May 1993).

———. *The Truth about Homosexuality: The Cry of the Faithful* (San Francisco: Ignatius Press, 1996).

Hildebrand, Dietrich von. *The Encyclical Humanae Vitae: A Sign of Contradiction* (Chicago: Franciscan Herald Press, 1969).

———. *In Defence of Purity* (New York: Sheed & Ward, 1935).

John Jay College of Criminal Justice. *The Nature and Scope of the Problem of Sexual Abuse of Minors by Catholic Priests and Deacons in the United States* [2004] (http://usccb.org/comm/mediarelations.shtml).

John Paul II. Homily Commemorating the Restorations of Michelangelo's Frescoes in the Sistine Chapel, April 8, 1994 (http://www.vatican.va/holy_father/john_paul_ii/homilies/1994/documents/hf_jpii_hom_1994048_restauri-sistina_en.html).

———. *Man and Woman He Created Them: A Theology of the Body*. Trans. Michael Waldstein (Boston: Pauline Books & Media, 2006).

———. *The Theology of the Body: Human Love in the Divine Plan* (Boston: Pauline Books & Media, 1997).

———. (Karol Wojtyla). *Love and Responsibility*. Trans. H. T. Willetts (San Francisco: Ignatius Press, 1993).

Jone, Fr. Heribert. *Moral Theology*. Trans. and adapted Fr. Urban Adelman, O.F.M. Cap. [1961] (Rockford, IL: Tan Books and Publishers, 1993).

Kippley, John F. *Sex and the Marriage Covenant: A Basis for Morality*, Second Edition (San Francisco: Ignatius Press, 2005).

Kosnik, Anthony, et al., editors. *Human Sexuality: New Directions in American Catholic Thought* (New York: Paulist Press, 1977).

Lawler, Rev. Ronald, O.F.M. Cap., Joseph Boyle, Jr., and William E. May. *Catholic Sexual Ethics: A Summary, Explanation, & Defense,* Second Edition (Huntington, IN: Our Sunday Visitor, 1998).

Loverde, Bishop Paul S. *Bought with a Price: Pornography and the Attack on the Living Temple of God* (2006). www.arlingtondiocese.org/offices/communications/boughtprice.html.

Marriage: Papal Teachings, selected by the Benedictine Monks of Solesmes. Trans. Michael J. Byrnes, (Boston: Daughters of St. Paul, 1963).

Mast, Coleen Kelly. *Love and Life: A Christian Sexual Morality for Teens* (San Francisco, Ignatius Press, 1986).

May, William E. *Marriage: The Rock on Which the Family Is Built* (San Francisco: Ignatius Press, 1995).

―――. *An Introduction to Moral Theology,* Second Edition (Huntington, IN: Our Sunday Visitor, 2003).

―――. "L'amore fra uomo e donna: archetipo di amore per eccellenza." In *La via dell'amore: Riflessioni sull'enciclica "Deus caritas est: di Benedetto XVI,"* edited by Livio Melina and Carl Anderson (Rome: Pontificio Instituto Giovanni Paolo II per Studi su matrimonio e famiglia, 2006), pp. 47–58.

―――. "*Humanae Vitae* at 40: Abundant Contemporary Literature from the Social Sciences Confirms Paul VI's Warnings about Contraception." *The Catholic World Report* (July 2008): 40-46.

McDermott, John M., S.J. "Science, Sexual Morality, and Church Teaching: Another Look at *Humanae Vitae*." *Irish Theological Quarterly* 70 (2005): 237–261.

―――. "Charles Curran's Moral Theory: Foundational Sexual Ethics." *Anthropotes* 07/ XXIII/1, 167–226.

Nathanson, Bernard, M.D., with Richard Ostling. *Aborting America* (Garden City, NY: Doubleday & Company, 1979).

Neuner, J., S.J., and J. Dupuis, S.J., eds. *The Christian Faith in the Doctrinal Documents of the Catholic Church*, Revised Edition (New York: Alba House, 1982).

Origins, vol. 15, no. 41 (Nov. 27, 1986), 669. "Some Background on Father Curran's Case."

Nicolosi, Joseph J. *Reparative Therapy of Male Homosexuality: A New Clinical Approach* (Lanham, MD: Jason Aronson Publishers, 2002).

Quian, Shao-Zhen. "China Successfully Launching Billings Ovulation Method." *Bulletin of the Ovulation Method Research and Reference Centre of Australia*, 30, 2 (June 2003).

Ott, Ludwig. *The Fundamentals of Catholic Dogma*. Trans. Patrick Lynch (St. Louis: B. Herder Book Company, 1958).

Ouellet, Marc Cardinal. *Divine Likeness: Toward a Trinitarian Anthropology of the Family*. Trans. Philip Milligan and Linda Cicone (Grand Rapids, MI and Cambridge, UK: William B. Eerdmans Publishing Company, 2006).

Parmisano, Fabian, O.P. "Love and Marriage in the Middle Ages II." *New Blackfriars*, vol. 50, no. 592 (September 1969): 649–66.

Peters, Edward, J.D., J.C.D. *Annulments and the Catholic Church* (West Chester, PA: Ascension Press, 2004).

Pontifical Council for the Family. *Enchiridion on the Family: A Compendium of Church Teaching on Family and Life Issues from Vatican II to the Present* (Boston: Pauline Books & Media, 2004).

Pontifical Council for Justice and Peace. *Compendium of the Social Doctrine of the Catholic Church* (USCCB Publishing, 2005).

Popenoe, David, and Barbara Whitehead. "The State of Our Unions: The Social Health of Marriage in America in 2005" *National Marriage Project* (New Brunswick, NJ: Rutgers University, 2005).

Provan, Charles. *The Bible and Birth Control* (Monongahela, PA: Zimmer Printing, 1989).

Prümmer, Dominic, O.P, *Handbook of Moral Theology*. Trans. J.G. Nolan (New York: P.J. Kenedy & Sons, 1957).

Quay, Paul M., S.J. "Contraception and Conjugal Love." *Theological Studies* 22 (1961).

———. *The Christian Meaning of Human Sexuality* (San Francisco: Ignatius Press, 1988).

Shivanandan, Mary. *Natural Sex* (New York: Rawson, Wade, 1979).

———. *Crossing the Threshold of Love: A New Vision of Marriage in the Light of Pope John Paul II's Anthropology* (Washington, DC: The Catholic University of America Press, 1999).

Smith Janet E. *Humanae Vitae: A Generation Later* (Washington, DC: Catholic University of America Press, 1991).

———, ed. *Why Humanae Vitae Was Right: A Reader* (San Francisco: Ignatius Press, 1993).

———. "The Connection between Contraception and Abortion." *Homiletic and Pastoral Review* (April 1993), 10–18.

Smith, Janet E., and Christopher Kaczor. *Life Issues, Medical Choices: Questions and Answers for Catholics* (Cincinnati, OH: Servant Books, 2007).

Stelton Leo F. *Dictionary of Ecclesiastical Latin* (Peabody, MA: Hendrickson Publishers, 1995).

Tanner, Norman P., S.J., ed. *The Decrees of the Ecumenical Councils, Volume II (Trent-Vatican II)* (London and Washington, DC: Sheed & Ward and Georgetown University Press, 1990).

Tapia, Ralph J. "Human Sexuality: The Magisterium and the Moral Theologians." *Thought*, vol. 54, no. 215 (December 1979), 405-418.

Thiel, John E. "Tradition and Reasoning: A Nonfoundationalist Perspective." *Theological Studies* 56 (December 1995), 627-651.

Treas, Judith, and Deidre Giesen. "Sexual Infidelity among Married and Cohabitating Americans." *Journal of Marriage and the Family*, vol. 62, no. 1 (February 2000), 48–60.

U.S. Conference of Catholic Bishops. *United States Catholic Catechism for Adults* (Washington, DC: U.S. Conference of Catholic Bishops, 2006).

U.S. Conference of Catholic Bishops Committee on Doctrine. *Ministry to Persons with a Homosexual Inclination: Guidelines for Pastoral Care*, November 14, 2006 (Washington, DC: USCCB, 2006).

Viviano, Benedict T. "The Gospel According to Matthew." In *The New Jerome Biblical Commentary*, ed. Raymond E. Brown et al. (Englewood Cliffs, NJ: Prentice Hall, 1990), no. 42:31-32, pp. 642-643.

Ware, Timothy (Bishop Kallistos of Diokleia). *The Orthodox Church,* New Edition (London: Penguin Books, 1993).

West, Christopher. *Good News About Sex & Marriage*, Revised Edition (Cincinnati, OH: St. Anthony Messenger Press, 2004).

Wetzel, Richard, M.D. *Sexual Wisdom: A Guide for Parents, Young Adults, Educators and Physicians* (Ann Arbor, MI: Proctor Publications, 1998).

Wilcox, W. Bradford. *Why Marriage Matters: Twenty-Six Conclusions from the Social Sciences*, 2nd Edition (New York: Institute for American Values, 2005).

Witham, Larry. *Curran vs. Catholic University: A Study of Authority and Freedom in Conflict* (Riverdale, MD: Edington-Rand, Inc., 1991).

Wolfe, Christopher, ed. *Same-Sex Matters: The Challenge of Homosexuality* (Dallas, TX: Spence Publishing Company, 2000).

Wood, Steve. *Breaking Free: 12 Steps to Sexual Purity for Men* [pamphlet] (Port Charlotte, FL: Family Life Center, 2002).

Zalba, Marcellinus. *Theologiae Moralis Summa* II (Madrid: Biblioeteca de Autores Cristianos, 1957).

Web Sites

Battle for Purity (Dr. Edward Sri)
www.infodesk@holyspiritinteractive.net

Catholic Medical Association
www.cathmed.org

Christian Alliance for Sexual Recovery
www.helpandhope.org

Couple to Couple League
www.ccli.org

Courage (spiritual support for Catholics struggling with homosexual tendencies)
www.couragerc.net

Family Life Center International (Steve Wood)
www.familylifecenter.net

John and Sheila Kippley (natural family planning information)
www.NFPandmore.org

Love Matters (Coleen Kelly Mast)
www.lovematters.com

Marriage Encounter
www.fwwme.org

Ministry of the North American Conference of Separated and Divorced Catholics
http://www.nacsdc.org

National Association for Research and Therapy of Homosexuality (NARTH)
www.narth.com

Pope Paul VI Institute for the Study of Human Reproduction, Omaha, NE
www.popepaulvi.com

Real Love Production (Mary Beth Bonacci)
www.reallove.net

Retrouvaille (for healing troubled marriages)
www.retrouvaille.org

Sexaholics Anonymous (SA)
www.sa.org

Sexual Common Sense (outstanding resources of Dr. Janet E.
Smith on contraception and other sexual topics)
www.mycatholicfaith

USCCB Natural Family Planning Office
NFP@usccb.org

USCCB Secretariat for Family, Laity, Women, and Youth
www.usccb.org/laity/marriage

INDEX

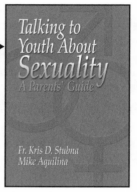